Cambridge Elements

Elements in New Religious Movements
Series Editor
Rebecca Moore
San Diego State University
Founding Editor
†James R. Lewis
Wuhan University

MORMONISM

Matthew Bowman
Claremont Graduate University

CAMBRIDGE
UNIVERSITY PRESS

Shaftesbury Road, Cambridge CB2 8EA, United Kingdom

One Liberty Plaza, 20th Floor, New York, NY 10006, USA

477 Williamstown Road, Port Melbourne, VIC 3207, Australia

314–321, 3rd Floor, Plot 3, Splendor Forum, Jasola District Centre,
New Delhi – 110025, India

103 Penang Road, #05–06/07, Visioncrest Commercial, Singapore 238467

Cambridge University Press is part of Cambridge University Press & Assessment,
a department of the University of Cambridge.

We share the University's mission to contribute to society through the pursuit of
education, learning and research at the highest international levels of excellence.

www.cambridge.org
Information on this title: www.cambridge.org/9781009537674

DOI: 10.1017/9781009537650

When citing this work, please include a reference to the DOI 10.1017/9781009537650

First published 2024

A catalogue record for this publication is available from the British Library.

ISBN 978-1-009-53767-4 Hardback
ISBN 978-1-009-53769-8 Paperback
ISSN 2635-232X (online)
ISSN 2635-2311 (print)

Mormonism

Elements in New Religious Movements

DOI: 10.1017/9781009537650
First published online: November 2024

Matthew Bowman
Claremont Graduate University

Author for correspondence: Matthew Bowman, matthewbbowman@gmail.com

Abstract: This Element will focus on the various denominations in the Mormon tradition, collectively sometimes referred to as "Mormonism." They include the Church of Jesus Christ of Latter-day Saints as well as the several sects of Mormon fundamentalism and multiple other denominations. Often described as the quintessential new religious movement, Mormonism is useful for studying the dynamics of new religious formation, evolution, schism, and adaptation to American culture more broadly. It emerged in the heat of the Second Great Awakening, the flourishing of religious creativity and innovation that followed American disestablishment, inspired by the visionary ideas of Joseph Smith Jr., a New York farmer who adopted a particular style of restorationism, a form of Christianity popular in the period. Since that time, the various branches of Mormonism have embraced different relationships with the broader stream of American culture. Some have sought integration with America's Protestant majority; others have emphasized sectarian distinctiveness.

Keywords: Mormonism, Joseph Smith, Church of Jesus Christ of Latter-day Saints, Fundamentalism, Modernism

ISBNs: 9781009537674 (HB), 9781009537698 (PB), 9781009537650 (OC)
ISSNs: 2635-232X (online), 2635-2311 (print)

Contents

1 Introduction

The Mormon tradition is among the best known of new religious movements that have appeared in the United States. Emerging in the early nineteenth century, in a world of combat among Protestant denominations and competition among revivalists, it has consistently taken on a denominational cast. Its major branches envision themselves as "churches," mirroring the emphasis on doctrine, ecclesiology, and priestly leadership characteristic of many Protestant denominations.

Several dozen churches belong to the Mormon tradition, which we might define as those that trace their origins to the career of Joseph Smith Jr. (Some prefer "Restorationist" or "Latter Day Saint" tradition.) Of these, the largest and best known is the Church of Jesus Christ of Latter-day Saints (LDS church) headquartered since 1847 in Salt Lake City, Utah. As of 2023, it claimed approximately seventeen million members around the world – slightly under half of those inside the United States. But there are a number of other Mormon churches as well, including the quarter-million-strong Community of Christ, which was organized in 1860 and from 1872 to 2001 was known as the Reorganized Church of Jesus Christ of Latter Day Saints. Also well known is the Fundamentalist Church of Jesus Christ of Latter-day Saints, which traces its history to a schism from the LDS church in the early twentieth century and has approximately 6,000 members. A number of other Mormon churches exist as well; for instance, the Church of Jesus Christ (Bickertonite) and the Church of Christ (Temple Lot), though the LDS church and Community of Christ are by far the largest. The spectrum of these movements shows the diverse ways Christianity itself might be envisioned, and the complicated politics surrounding non-Protestant movements in the United States.

Therefore, I use "Mormon" to refer to the religious tradition that includes all of these movements, including the movement during Joseph Smith's lifetime. After Smith's death I refer to the "Latter-day Saint" or "LDS" church, as that which Brigham Young headed and moved to Salt Lake City; the "Reorganized," "RLDS" or eventually "Community of Christ" church, that which was organized under the leadership of Joseph Smith III in 1860; and finally the "fundamentalist movement," which emerged in the 1920s, and its most-studied denomination, the "FLDS" or "Fundamentalist Church of Jesus Christ of Latter-Day Saints." I explore these three among the various Mormon denominations because they represent a spectrum of assimilation to the broadly Protestant culture of the United States, ranging from great comfort to much resistance. These three traditions, then, illustrate the range of possibilities for Mormonism in the nation.

This Element first discusses the history of the Mormon movement, emphasizing its origins as a restorationist Christian movement, one which maintained that genuine Christianity had vanished and required renewal. However, Mormonism's distinctive restorationism and its collisions with American government and culture led to a series of schisms. I will then survey the beliefs and practices of the three branches of the movement noted earlier, emphasizing how their particular interpretations of Mormonism emerge from the career of Joseph Smith Jr., but also how they responded to the cultural and political pressures of the United States in different ways.

A survey of the historiography of Mormonism follows. Scholarship on the Mormon denominations emerged from the denominations themselves, and often initially reflected those denominations' priorities and self-conceptions. However, as it has evolved over time, that scholarship has come to reflect broader trends in the academy, and has shifted toward the exploration of how Mormonism might illustrate how the category of religion functions within the United States. The diversity of movements within the Mormon tradition can be read as a variety of responses to the modes by which the American state and the bulk of its population conceived of "genuine" religion. The differing expressions of the various Mormon churches, then, reveal how a new religious movement might seek to establish an identity in resistance to or in accommodation with these expectations.

2 Joseph Smith and the First Mormons

The religious career of Joseph Smith Jr. (1805–1944) and the Mormon churches that grew from it are rooted in Christian restorationism. A number of scholars have pointed out the significance of the Smith family background for the character of Mormon restorationism.[1] The Smith family, Joseph Smith Sr. and Lucy Mack Smith and their eleven children, were Puritan-descended on both sides. Joseph Sr. was born in Topsfield, Massachusetts; Lucy Mack in New Hampshire. They married in 1796, and Joseph Smith Jr., their fourth child, was born in Sharon, Vermont, in 1805. Joseph Smith Sr. moved his family back and forth across New England seeking a sustainable profession. By 1816, the family had settled on a farm just outside Palmyra, New York.

The Smiths lived in a world of religious disestablishment. The collapse of state-sponsored religious organizations that followed the American Revolution ended with a Massachusetts state law in 1833. This process paralleled another, a long period of growth of new Christian movements scholars have called the

---

[1] On Smith's life the best biography is Richard Lyman Bushman, *Joseph Smith: Rough Stone Rolling* (New York: Knopf, 2005).

Second Great Awakening. In places like Palmyra, the ragged frontier of the white population of the United States, the strong Christian ecclesiastical organizations of Puritan New England, or Anglican Britain did not exist. Instead, there emerged the Methodists and Baptists, revival-driven denominations that leaned on lay charismatic preaching and were often suspicious of trained ministers who graduated from seminaries. Even the older denominations like the Presbyterians felt the pressure of these movements and adopted some revivalist qualities – emotional meetings, impromptu preaching, and what has been called the plain style of reading the Bible. This style dismissed the notion that one needed an education or knowledge of ancient languages to properly understand what the Bible was saying. Instead, like all knowledge, it was comprehensible to anybody with common faculties.[2]

The Smiths, like many of these Christians, were unchurched, but were descended from Puritans on both sides, were Bible readers, and considered themselves Christians. Joseph Smith's mother Lucy Mack Smith came from a visionary family; many of her siblings had powerful spiritual experiences that confirmed to them that Jesus Christ had saved them. In Palmyra she and several of the children sought a church home, eventually joining the Presbyterian church. Joseph Smith Sr. was less interested, though not because he did not believe. He had visionary dreams and spoke of valuing the original religion of Jesus, which he did not hold was on the earth at that time.[3]

Joseph Smith Jr thus grew up in a family with restorationist leanings. Many antebellum American Protestant Christians, with limited experience with and interest in the churches of the day, believed it necessary to restore original biblical Christianity, which they did not believe currently existed. Often these restorationists were Christians descended from the English Puritans, who believed that the best way to restore original Christianity was to strip away all the barnacles of ritual and practice and theology that had latched onto the hull of the Christian ship. This was true, for instance, for Alexander Campbell (1788–1866) and Barton Stone (1772–1844), founders of the Disciples of Christ and contemporaries of Joseph Smith whose ideas were widely influential. Many antebellum Baptist and nondenominational Christian churches sought to achieve something similar, founding simple, plain churches that required little

---

[2] William G. McLoughlin, *Revivals, Awakenings and Reform* (Chicago, IL: University of Chicago Press, 2013), 107–12; Amanda Porterfield, *Conceived in Doubt: Religion and Politics in the New American Nation* (Chicago, IL: University of Chicago, 2012), 155–56; George Marsden, "Everyone One's Own Interpreter? The Bible, Science, and Authority in Mid-Nineteenth Century America," *History of Education Quarterly* 17 (Spring 1977), 17–30.

[3] Lavina Fielding Anderson, ed., *Lucy's Book: A Critical Edition of Lucy Mack Smith's Family Memoir* (Salt Lake City, UT: Signature Books, 2001), 296–98.

more than a pulpit and a Bible. They spurned what they deemed excessive ritual, liturgy, and decoration.[4]

Much of this work reflected impulses widely shared among American Protestants influenced by the British Puritans, who spurned features found in other Christian traditions, like Roman Catholicism or the Church of England, such as elaborate art and architecture, extensive and complex music, special clothing, and ritual for services. Instead, they emphasized plainness and simplicity. Their worship focused almost entirely on Bible reading and sermonizing. Some such groups would only sing the Psalms of the Hebrew Bible itself, spurning any modern hymnody.

At the same time, many other groups believed that the restoration of biblical Christianity required expansion. New text, new revelation, new ritual; the reenactment of first-century spiritual gifts like speaking in tongues or miraculous healing; the reemergence of biblical designations like priest or prophet. Charismatic groups began speaking in tongues. Mother Ann Lee (1736–1784), leader of the Shaker movement, declared herself a reincarnation of Jesus Christ, and her movement embraced ecstatic ritual, dancing, bodily contortion, singing in unknown languages, and rolling about. The New York visionary Robert Matthews (1778–1841) believed he was the biblical apostle Matthias reborn. Multiple groups, like the incipient Seventh-day Adventists and the Shakers, produced new revelatory texts. Jemima Wilkinson (1752–1819), calling herself the Public Universal Friend, dictated divine revelations "as was done in the days of the prophets of old," as one follower put it. Ellen Gould White (1827–1915), who became a prophetic figure to the Adventist movement, wrote vast volumes of revelations of which one follower declared, "Sister White is not the originator of these books. They contain the instruction that during her lifetime God has been giving her." Restoration, then, could take on a variety of forms.[5]

---

[4] C. Leonard Allen and Richard T. Hughes discuss these sorts of restorationists in *Illusions of Innocence: Protestant Primitivism in America, 1630–1875* (Chicago, IL: University of Chicago Press, 1988).

[5] David F. Holland, *Sacred Borders: Continuing Revelation and Canonical Restraint in Early America* (New York: Oxford University Press, 2011); Paul Conkin, *Cane Ridge: America's Pentecost* (Madison, WI: University of Wisconsin Press, 1990); and Robert Abzug, *Cosmos Crumbling: American Reform and the Religious Imagination* (New York: Oxford University Press, 1994), all emphasize restoration as the creation of new scripture, practices, and new forms of life. Shaker practices are described in Stephen J. Stein, *The Shaker Experience in America* (New Haven, CT: Yale University Press, 1992), 16–19. Wilkinson's follower cited in Paul B. Moyer, *The Public Universal Friend: Jemima Wilkinson and Religious Enthusiasm in Revolutionary America* (Ithaca, NY: Cornell University Press, 2015), 72. Arthur White cited in Arthur Patrick, "Author," in Terrie Aamodt, Gary Land, and Ronald L. Numbers, eds., *Ellen Harmon White: American Prophet* (New York: Oxford University Press, 2008), 92.

Joseph Smith's movement fell into the latter camp. As the religious studies scholar Jan Shipps observed, Smith sought to blend the Hebrew Bible and the New Testament, to stand high priests and prophets next to apostles and disciples and build the temples and tabernacles of Moses and Solomon next to the house churches of Paul.[6] Later in his life, Joseph Smith described experiencing a series of visions in his youth. The first, sometime in his teenage years, describes an encounter with God and Jesus Christ. The sources that describe this vision date to the 1830s and place the date somewhat differently. This sort of vision was not entirely unique in early antebellum America; a number of Christians at the time described such encounters that resembled Smith's own. God and Christ reassured the worried mortal about the salvation of their soul. By the time Smith was an adult, though, he credited this vision with another thing as well: he emerged from it convinced that no Christian group on earth was practicing Christianity correctly, and that a restoration of biblical Christianity was necessary.[7] This restoration would innovate in a number of ways, creating new priesthood hierarchies, new scripture, and new ritual.

The Prophetic Career of Joseph Smith

Throughout the 1820s Smith claimed he experienced a series of encounters with an angel who directed him to a set of plates bound together by metal rings buried in a hill near his home. Smith said that these plates contained the records of an ancient civilization. Under the charismatic influence of the Holy Spirit and using the tools of folk magic – seerstones and divination – familiar to common folk throughout the Anglo-American world, Smith translated the writings on these plates and in 1829 published the results as the Book of Mormon.

The Book of Mormon is a quarter-million-word-long narrative written in English reminiscent of the King James Bible Smith was familiar with. It purports to be the record of an ancient civilization in the Americas founded by Israelite refugees from the Babylonian conquest of Jerusalem in the 590s BCE. It is written in the voices of multiple leaders of this civilization over the course of a thousand years. Having been led to a new land by God, these people divide into rival nations called the Nephites and the Lamanites, respectively. In their religion they mirror the complex restorationism of the later Mormon movement. The book's narrators revere the prophet Isaiah, the Law of Moses, and the House of Israel. And yet, they are resolutely Christian as well, describing Jesus by name before his birth and insisting that the Hebrew prophets

---

[6] Jan Shipps, *Mormonism: The Story of a New Religious Tradition* (Urbana, IL: University of Illinois Press, 1985), 51–3.

[7] Stephen C. Harper, *First Vision: Memory and Mormon Origins* (New York: Oxford University Press, 2019).

testified of Jesus's miracles and divine nature. At the climax of the book, the resurrected Jesus Christ appears to these people and establishes his church among them.[8] In theology, the Book of Mormon's Christian teachings resemble Protestantism, emphasizing the incapacity of human beings to save themselves, the merciful atonement of Jesus Christ, and teaching the importance of baptism and the Lord's Supper.

In its attempt to reconcile the Hebrew Bible and the New Testament, the book might be read as a model for Smith himself. After publishing the Book of Mormon he claimed the mantle of prophet, citing as his models Isaiah and Moses. In 1830 he organized a church, which he led for fourteen years until his assassination in 1844. In 1830 he called it the Church of Christ. Eight years later he changed its name to the Church of Jesus Christ of Latter-day Saints. He marked the new faith with offices, practices, and traditions drawn both from the Hebrew Bible and the New Testament.

Smith initially populated the church with the same sort of ministerial offices as many Protestant churches at the time – deacons, bishops, teachers and the like, all named in the New Testament. But by the mid-1830s, he began speaking of priesthood, an authority that overlapped all of these offices. He cited the Hebrew Bible figures Aaron, the brother of Moses who became the first Israelite priest, and the shadowy figure Melchizedek from the book of Genesis, who, Smith said, echoing the Epistle to the Hebrews, held a "high priesthood." Smith said that each priesthood, that of Aaron and Melchizedek, was restored to him by resurrected New Testament figures – Peter, James and John and John the Baptist. Ecclesiastical offices like deacon, teacher, and priest were sorted into either the Aaronic or the Melchizedek priesthoods. By the early 1830s Smith ordained every man who joined his church to the priesthood and assigned to them some office.[9]

Later he added the office of patriarch, inspired by the Book of Genesis figures Abraham, Isaac, and Jacob, and twelve apostles, modeled on the closest disciples of Jesus in the Gospels and the Acts of the Apostles. He built temples in Kirtland, Ohio, and Nauvoo, Illinois, in which he instituted ritual practices

---

[8] On the emergence of the Book of Mormon and its hybrid theology, see Terryl Givens, *By the Hand of Mormon: The American Scripture that Launched a New World Religion* (New York: Oxford University Press, 2002), particularly 185–209 on the Book of Mormon's high Christology embedded in the context of the Hebrew Bible; Michael Austin, *Testimony of Two Nations: How the Book of Mormon Reads, and Rereads, the Bible* (Urbana, IL: University of Illinois Press, 2024); and Joseph M. Spencer, *A Word in Season: Isaiah's Reception in the Book of Mormon* (Urbana, IL: University of Illinois Press, 2023).

[9] On the formulation and creation of priesthood, see Jonathan Stapley, *The Power of Godliness: Mormon Liturgy and Cosmology* (New York: Oxford University Press, 2018) and Michael Hubbard MacKay, *Prophetic Authority: Democratic Hierarchy and the Mormon Priesthood* (Urbana, IL: University of Illinois Press, 2020).

inspired by the Bible. He embraced some charismatic practices described in the epistles of Paul, like healing, prophecy, and to a certain extent speaking in tongues. And most famously, he reinstituted polygamy.

A number of scholars have observed that Smith's restoration of biblical practices accelerated as his career went on.[10] The church began in the neighborhood of Smith's home in Palmyra, New York, and moved to Kirtland, Ohio, near Cleveland, at the end of 1830. Smith took his followers to Kirtland to join the congregation of Sidney Rigdon (1793–1876), a popular restorationist Baptist preacher and associate of Alexander Campbell. Rigdon and his entire congregation had been converted by missionaries Joseph Smith had sent out bearing the Book of Mormon, and Rigdon's people more than doubled the size of the small church. While he was in Ohio, Smith dictated several revelations that embraced the notion of economic communalism and universal salvation. This version of Mormon restorationism emphasized the New Testament, following Rigdon's group, and presented a Christianity that attempted to replicate that as described in the Acts of the Apostles.

By the mid-1830s, though, Smith's ideas were moving steadily toward incorporating more of the Hebrew Bible. In 1836 he dedicated a temple in Kirtland, announcing it was modeled on the temple of King Solomon. He also began to discuss "Zion," a concept described in the prophetic and historical books of the Hebrew Bible. It means a specific place – most often Jerusalem – but also a concept; a holy site where God will commune with and protect his people. In 1831, Joseph Smith dictated a series of revelations indicating that Zion was to be found near Independence, Missouri. There, Smith said, a New Jerusalem would be built around a series of temples. This Zion site was where Adam and Eve lived after departing the Garden of Eden, and it was also where Jesus Christ would descend when he returned to the earth at the end of times.

Accordingly, Joseph Smith and his followers began to purchase land in and around Independence, Missouri, and Mormon converts began to settle there. But both the Kirtland and the Missouri settlements were torn apart. In both places, the church began to behave as something other than a Protestant denomination, adopting practices beyond the restorationist theology of Alexander Campbell or other reformist groups. Purchasing land, building temples, instituting ritualized practices there, gathering the entire group of believers in a single location—these were things unfamiliar to Protestants. Many of Joseph Smith's converts objected.[11]

---

[10] See, for instance, Bushman, *Rough Stone Rolling*, 216–18.

[11] Overviews of the Kirtland and Missouri periods of Mormon history include Mark Staker, *Hearken, O Ye People: The Historical Setting of Joseph Smith's Ohio Revelations* (Salt Lake

In the mid-1830s, Smith took three steps that moved his tradition past Protestantism. First, he began to produce more scripture. Beyond simply producing the Book of Mormon, he and Rigdon began to revise the Bible. Smith claimed that divine revelation informed him of the gaps, mistranslations, and errors or lacunae in the biblical manuscripts that required correcting. While in Kirtland he purchased, improbably, two Egyptian mummies and several ancient papyri from a traveling showman and identified the papyri as containing writings of the patriarch Abraham. He proceeded to translate these, he said, through divine revelation. In this process he produced two new complete works of scripture – the Book of Abraham and the Book of Moses. Of course, Smith had little expertise in ancient languages, and modern scholars have identified the papyri as containing common Egyptian funerary texts. What Smith meant by "translating," then, is open to interpretation. Some scholars have concluded Smith engaged in conscious deception; others link Smith's projects to well-documented visionary experiences connected to language, like glossolalia.[12]

Second, Smith instituted the Law of Consecration. He designated several church officials to be "bishops," and directed that all church members should turn over their property to the bishops, who would distribute it according to the need of all members. Many Protestant restorationist groups practiced similar efforts at economic communalism, following the description in the Acts of the Apostles of the early Christian church, which held all things in common (Acts 2:44–47 and 4:32–37). Indeed, Smith encountered one upon the move to Ohio. Several families in Rigdon's congregations had pooled their properties and were attempting to live an economically communalist lifestyle.[13]

In both Ohio and Missouri, members of the church pursued the Law of Consecration, extending it not only to the pooling of property but also to the formation of church-operated businesses. Such efforts interwove with Joseph Smith's hope to bind his followers together physically. Converts to the Mormon movement began to gather in Ohio and Missouri, around the leaders and sacred sites of their faith. In Missouri, church members and Smith himself purchased large swaths of land around the location of Zion. In Ohio, Smith attempted to charter a bank, hoping it would boost the economy of Kirtland and provide a strong base upon which he might finance a temple. When the Ohio legislature

---

City, UT: Greg Kofford Books, 2011), and Stephen LeSeuer, *The 1838 Mormon War in Missouri* (Columbia, MO: University of Missouri Press, 2011).

[12] Samuel Morris Brown, *Joseph Smith's Translations: The Words and Worlds of Early Mormonism* (New York: Oxford University Press, 2020), is the most thorough exploration of Smith's translations, evaluating both the content and the methodology of the process.

[13] The best study of these practices is Leonard J. Arrington, Dean L. May, and Feramorz Fox, *Building the Kingdom of God: Community and Cooperation among the Mormons* (Urbana, IL: University of Illinois Press, 1992).

refused to issue a charter, citing the lack of relevant experience among the Mormon leadership, Smith went ahead anyway, calling the effort an Anti-Banking Society, and encouraged members to purchase shares.

Lastly, Smith built a temple. At the dedication of the Kirtland temple in March 1836, Smith began to institute ritual practices foreign to most Protestant Christians in the United States. In the Kirtland temple Mormons washed each other ritually and then anointed each other with oil, imitating the priestly practices described in the books of Exodus and Leviticus, and the footwashing Jesus performs in the gospels (John 13:1–5). These practices foretold those which would come later. While his second temple rose in Nauvoo, Illinois, Smith instituted far more elaborate rites modeled upon Masonic initiation rituals.[14]

All of these efforts generated hostility from within and without the church. Almost as soon as Joseph Smith organized his church, there was dissension and disagreement about what Mormonism should look like, what the role of its leaders should be, and what its appropriate practices were. As Joseph Smith himself moved from New York to Kirtland, Ohio, to Independence, Missouri, and then to Nauvoo, Illinois, he left behind others who claimed that Mormonism was something other than what Joseph Smith himself claimed.

In both Kirtland and Missouri the new church attracted opposition from non-Mormon neighbors. In Missouri in particular, the large number of new Mormon migrants – thousands by the middle of the decade – to the areas around Independence caused worry, for several reasons. First, the Law of Consecration meant that the Mormons kept to themselves economically. They purchased much land, they traded among themselves, and were seen as a drag on local economic development. Second, the Mormons tended to vote as a bloc. Finally, their population was growing rapidly, largely from migration, and largely from the North. In an era of increasing sectional crisis, white Missourians did not trust northern converts – a fear exacerbated when a Mormon journalist published an article in a church newspaper stating that the Mormon gospel would be preached to people of all races.

Over the course of the 1830s, a series of mobs drove the Mormons to northern Missouri and away from Independence in 1833. In Kirtland, Ohio, five years later, the Anti-Banking Society failed, and in the tumult that followed, many Mormons – including Joseph Smith himself – fled to the Mormon settlements north of Independence. But that fall, when a mob attempted to prevent Mormons from voting in Gallatin, Missouri, conflict broke out. Joseph Smith rallied

---

[14] Michael Homer, *Joseph's Temples: The Dynamic Relationship between Freemasonry and Mormonism* (Salt Lake City, UT: University of Utah Press, 2014).

a private Mormon militia; in response, a private Missouri militia demanded that the Mormons abandon their settlements. Missourians began to burn Mormon homes, and the Mormon militia responded by raiding other settlements.

In late October several dozen Mormon militiamen clashed with a similar-sized company of the Missouri militia. Four died, including David Patten (1799–1838), a high-ranking Mormon leader. In response, Lilburn Boggs (1796–1860), governor of Missouri, issued Executive Order 44, directing the state government to drive the Mormons from the state. On October 30, a group of Missouri militiamen killed eighteen Mormons, including women and children, at the settlement of Haun's Mill. Joseph Smith directed the church to retreat to Illinois, and he himself surrendered to Missouri state authorities.

But alongside this opposition from outsiders, in both Ohio and Missouri, significant figures in church leadership objected to the development of Smith's thought and practices. Some protested the church's interventions into the economy. When the Anti-Banking Society failed and many church members lost their investments, some declared Smith a fallen prophet. Similarly, others protested the idea of the Law of Consecration in the first place, arguing that Joseph Smith was attempting to seize the wealth of new members for himself. Others found Joseph Smith's continuing dictation of revelations puzzling and objected to their content. In Missouri, some of Joseph Smith's closest associates were excommunicated from the church after clashing with local Mormon leaders over property ownership in Zion. And after the fall of the Anti-Banking Society in Kirtland, Joseph Smith's secretary Warren Parrish (1803–1877) formed what he called the Church of Christ, which he said was a pure form of Mormonism dedicated to the theology of the Book of Mormon, and not Joseph Smith's later experiments in economics.

A similar process occurred in Nauvoo, Illinois. Joseph Smith bought a plot of land in a bend of the Mississippi River just on the Illinois border in 1839 and urged his followers to flee there. By that summer, approximately 10,000 had straggled across the river from Missouri, and Joseph Smith himself, out of a Missouri prison, joined them. In Nauvoo he continued his elaboration of restorationist thought and practice. Citing the passage in Genesis that describes human beings made in God's own image, Smith taught that God had a body; that God is simply an exalted human being, and that human beings can, over eons of moral and intellectual development, progress to Godhood themselves. He also greatly elaborated the temple ceremonies, having a temple built and instituting a rite called the endowment, a ritual drama of Adam and Eve's fall from the Garden of Eden and their journey back to God. He taught church members to participate in this ritual in order to make covenants with God. And he instituted polygamy, citing Abraham, Isaac, and Jacob as his model.[15]

These issues again divided Smith's followers. Polygamy, particularly, proved explosive. Smith kept it a secret as long as he could. He personally married some three dozen women in Nauvoo but openly acknowledged none as his wife. These women stayed with their families, and he visited them (when he visited, which was rarely) in private. But he also initiated several of his closest male followers into the practice, and slowly it spread across the city. By 1842 and 1843, rumors were rampant. Smith's first wife, Emma Hale Smith (1804–1879), whom he had married in 1827, sought to rally the Relief Society, the church's women's organization which she headed, against the rumors before discovering that they were true and clashing with her husband.[16]

In early 1844, one of Smith's highest lieutenants, William Law (1809–1892), broke with Smith over the practice and was excommunicated from the church. He formed what he called the True Church of Jesus Christ of Latter Day Saints and published a newspaper, the *Nauvoo Expositor*, wherein he denounced polygamy and labeled Smith a fallen prophet. Smith urged the city council to declare the newspaper a public nuisance that would stoke unrest and urged the destruction of its printing press. After the council complied and the press destroyed, public outrage spread through western Illinois. Fearing mob attacks on Nauvoo, Smith again marshaled a militia – the Nauvoo Legion, which had been duly chartered by the state government several years earlier. In response, the militia in the neighboring town of Carthage mobilized, and, fearing violence, the governor of Illinois intervened. Smith agreed to face charges of inciting a riot in the county seat of Carthage, and reported to the jail there on June 25, 1844, in the company of his brother Hyrum and two of the church's apostles. Two days later, a mob attacked the jail and killed both Smith brothers.

Schism

The death of Joseph Smith precipitated a crisis in the church. There were several overlapping communities within Mormonism at this point. The inner church, comprising several dozen of Joseph Smith's closest associates, had been fully initiated into the endowment ceremonies of the temple. Many knew of polygamy and some practiced it. This group was centered upon the Quorum of the Twelve Apostles, the church's chief missionaries, and Joseph Smith's best friends.

---

[15] On the religious innovations in Nauvoo see Benjamin Park, *Kingdom of Nauvoo: The Rise and Fall of a Religious Empire on the American Frontier* (New York: Liveright, 2020).

[16] Emma Hale Smith's work is discussed in Park, *Kingdom of Nauvoo*, and in the best biography of Smith, Linda King Newell and Valeen Tippetts Avery, *Mormon Enigma: Emma Hale Smith*, 2nd ed. (Urbana, IL: University of Illinois Press, 1994), 159–79.

The Quorum also held the trust of the hundreds of converts they had gained, mostly from mission work in Great Britain they had pursued in the previous several years – though many of these new members knew only rumors of polygamy and virtually nothing at all about the temple endowment ceremonies.[17]

Another faction surrounded the Smith family – Emma Smith, Joseph's widow, and his young children, his surviving brothers Samuel and William, and his elderly mother Lucy Mack. Smith had attempted to conceal polygamy from Emma, and though she had learned of it she never reconciled herself to the practice. She sought an alliance with William Marks (1792–1872), the head of the church's Nauvoo congregation and opposed the continuation of polygamy in the church.

Several of these figures sought to replace Joseph Smith at the head of the church over the long, hot summer of 1844. Emma Smith supported William Marks's bid. Brigham Young (1801–1877), leader of the Quorum of the Twelve Apostles, opposed Emma Smith and asserted that the apostles should lead the church. Sidney Rigdon, who after a dispute over polygamy had fallen from Smith's favor and returned to his home in Pennsylvania several months prior, returned to make his own case. Another claimant, James Strang (1813–1856), seemed Joseph Smith in miniature. A relatively new convert to the church, like Smith himself tall, young, and handsome, he claimed that upon Smith's demise an angel had appeared and told him he was God's designated replacement.

Over the six months following Smith's death, his church splintered into multiple Mormonisms, each claiming a different interpretation of his legacy and adopting a particular constellation of the ideas and practices and scriptures he had produced. Both Strang and Rigdon ended up founding churches of their own. Under the leadership of William Bickerton, followers of Rigdon eventually formed the Church of Christ in Monongahela, Pennsylvania, in 1862. They rejected the need for the temple endowment and polygamy, as well as the bulk of Joseph Smith's revelations as scripture, adopting the Bible and Book of Mormon and the bulk of the priesthood hierarchy Smith had created. The Church of Jesus Christ, as it is now called, has approximately 22,000 members, led by a church president, two counselors, and twelve apostles.[18]

---

[17] This formulation emerges from D. Michael Quinn, "The Mormon Succession Crisis of 1844," *BYU Studies* 16:2 (Winter 1976), 187–235; Benjamin Park and Robin Jensen, "Debating Succession, March 1846: John E. Page, Orson Hyde, and the Trajectories of Joseph Smith's Legacy," *Journal of Mormon History* 39:1 (Winter 2013), 181–205; Andrew Ehat, "Joseph Smith's Introduction of Temple Ordinances and the 1844 Succession Question," (M.A. thesis: Brigham Young University, 1982).

[18] After Rigdon, this church was reorganized and led by William Bickerton. See Daniel Stone, *William Bickerton: Forgotten Latter Day Prophet* (Salt Lake City, UT: Signature Books, 2018).

On the other hand, James Strang's Church of Jesus Christ of Latter Day Saints adopted virtually all of Smith's innovations. Strang produced new scripture from ancient metal plates, claimed visitation by angels, began the construction of a temple, and wielded a letter of appointment he claimed was written by Joseph Smith himself. For several months Strang gained the allegiance of more than 10,000 Mormons, including some of Smith's closest associates. However, when Strang began openly practicing polygamy at the end of the 1840s, many of those who had flocked to him abandoned his leadership. In another eerie parallel with Smith, Strang was assassinated in 1856 and his followers scattered, leaving his church with only a few hundred members by the end of the twentieth century.[19]

Despite their relative obscurity the movements Strang and Rigdon founded illustrate the diversity of possible Mormonisms that emerged after the trauma of Smith's death. Some larger Mormon movements, like the Reorganized Church of Jesus Christ of Latter Day Saints, sought to overcome American resistance to Mormon restorationism by increasingly accommodating the expectations of American culture, while others taught that the lesson of Smith's death was the corruption of American society, and the necessity of resistance to it.

3 Mormonisms

The most numerically successful expressions of Mormonism that took shape after the death of Smith are the Church of Jesus Christ of Latter-day Saints and the Reorganized Church of Jesus Christ of Latter Day Saints (now called Community of Christ). Both emerged in the mid-nineteenth century, shortly after Smith's own death. Several decades later, a third formulation, sometimes called Mormon fundamentalism, emerged. Its best-known manifestation is the Fundamentalist Church of Jesus Christ of Latter-day Saints. When put into comparison, these three movements illustrate differing forms of Mormon restorationism, particularly in relationship with broader American culture.[20] Hence, they show how new religious movements grapple with accommodation or resistance to American culture.

The Church of Jesus Christ of Latter-day Saints

The Church of Jesus Christ of Latter-day Saints emerged from the leadership of the Quorum of the Twelve Apostles, the high-ranking missionaries of Joseph

---

[19] Vicki Cleverly Speek, *God Has Made Us a Kingdom: James Strang and the Midwest Mormons* (Salt Lake City, UT: Signature Books, 2006).

[20] This comparison draws on the work of John-Charles Duffy and David Howlett, *Mormonism: The Basics* (New York: Routledge, 2016).

Smith's church who were close to Smith and initiated into all of the practices and beliefs he developed in Nauvoo, including polygamy and temple rituals. Led by the Quorum's president, former carpenter Brigham Young, the apostles quickly moved to assert control over the church's property and populace. Young called a conference of the church in August 1844 and presented his case for control of the church against Sidney Rigdon, James Strang, and the group around Emma Smith. A majority of church members present – many of them British converts who supported the Twelve – affirmed his leadership. Over the next few months he excommunicated many of his rivals—Strang, Rigdon, and various members of the Smith family among them—and set about spreading the version of Mormonism he believed Joseph Smith had taught. Upon completing construction of the Nauvoo temple, he opened the endowment ceremony to all members of the church. In 1846, convinced that persistent violence made Latter-day Saint existence in the United States impossible, he organized his followers and led them to the Salt Lake Valley in western North America, arriving in the summer of 1847. At the time, this land was occupied by the Shoshone, Ute, and Paiute peoples, and in early 1848 upon the conclusion of the Mexican American War became territory of the United States.[21]

Along the way, Young declared his intention to reorganize the presidency of the church, and he assumed that office in February 1847. Since that turning point, the LDS church has been organized under the leadership of a group of men (as the LDS church has always restricted ordination to its priesthood to men) referred to as the General Authorities. These consist of a president of the church with two counselors, referred to as the First Presidency. Below these three in seniority is the Quorum of the Twelve Apostles. All of these leaders serve for life; upon the death of the president of the church, the most senior apostle by length of service takes the office, as Brigham Young replaced Joseph Smith. The president's counselors are normally also drawn from the Quorum of the Twelve. Since the 1970s, a group of General Authorities referred to as "seventies" (from Jesus's call of seventy missionaries in Luke 10:1) have served as intermediaries between the Quorum of the Twelve and the local leadership of the church. At the local level, the church is organized into stakes, roughly the equivalent of a Catholic diocese. A stake is made up of several wards – local congregations of several hundred people each. A stake is led by a stake president and two counselors; a ward by a bishop and two counselors. At the local level, all church offices are filled by lay members of the ward or stake in question who serve part time. This was largely the

---

[21] On the migration west and Brigham Young's leadership, see Wallace Stegner, *The Gathering of Zion: The Story of the Mormon Trail* (Lincoln, NE: University of Nebraska Press, 1992); John G. Turner, *Brigham Young: Pioneer Prophet* (Cambridge, MA: Harvard University Press, 2012).

structure of the church that emerged in Utah under the leadership of Brigham Young and remains the same today.

Young's decision to depart the United States reflected his conviction that his version of Mormonism was no longer compatible with Protestant America. And, indeed, a great deal of scholarship has observed how many Protestants described what the Latter-day Saints were doing as something other than religion. They labeled it a tyranny, a deception, a new nation. They did this because Young emphasized those elements of Mormonism least like traditional Protestantism: polygamy, temple worship, ritual, and, increasingly, a communal vision of society derived from the law of consecration far from the Protestant perception of religion as voluntary membership in an independent congregation.[22]

The political, economic, and social organization of the Utah settlement was directed by the church, and bowing to the realities on the ground, the president of the United States appointed Brigham Young governor of the Utah territory. The settlement of the territory was largely organized and directed by the LDS leadership, which divided the land of the Utah territory among settlers. The notion of a ward – a geographic unit whose inhabitants formed a congregation led by an appointed bishop – emerged under Joseph Smith in Nauvoo, but proved critical in the Salt Lake Valley. Responsibility was placed by LDS leaders in each bishop's hands for directing irrigation, cultivation, and distribution of the land. Similarly, the LDS church formed a political party, the Peoples Party, and church leaders selected candidates for election to municipal and state offices. To many Protestant Americans, the Utah Territory quite quickly seemed to become a theocracy, which dredged up old fears of Roman Catholicism, Islam, and other movements American Protestants termed "despotisms" or "kingdoms," rather than religions. For Protestants, religion had to do with what one believed, and should not dictate issues like land ownership or political organization.[23]

The fear of theocracy melded with the most lurid image of the LDS church: the sight of one man with multiple wives. Under Brigham Young's leadership polygamy was made public and formally acknowledged, and became far more systematized than the ad hoc, secret practices of Nauvoo. Men rising in church leadership were especially encouraged to participate. Historians estimate that approximately one quarter of Latter-day Saints in the period between the settlement of the Salt Lake Valley and 1890, when the LDS leadership formally

---

[22] See, for instance, Spencer Fluhman, *A Peculiar People: Antimormonism and the Making of Religion in Nineteenth Century America* (Chapel Hill, NC: University of North Carolina Press, 2012).

[23] Josiah Strong, *Our Country: Its Possible Future and Present Crisis* (New York: American Home Missionary Society, 1885), 62, 67.

renounced the practice, were involved in polygamous families. The practice was monitored by LDS leaders, who approved or rejected possible marriages, encouraged certain men to enter the practice, and others to avoid it. The highest leaders of the Church had many wives. Brigham Young and his friend and counselor Heber C. Kimball (1801–1868) each had dozens of wives, though they were the exception; even among the apostles and certainly among local leaders of the church somewhere between two and ten was far more typical. Though many of these marriages were mere formalities – a way to provide a woman economic support, for instance – it was widely understood that polygamous marriages were genuine marriages, and both Young and Kimball had dozens of children.

LDS women widely experienced polygamy as a trial. Many mourned emotional alienation from husbands they rarely saw and unsought rivalries with other spouses. Often they found alternate sources of satisfaction and leadership in the Relief Society, the church's women's organization first led by Emma Smith, which was reconstituted in Utah and plunged into a variety of causes and activism – from relief work for the poor to education to advocating for women's suffrage. Thanks in part to Relief Society activism women voted in the Utah Territory as early as 1870. The Relief Society founded and operated a hospital, several official and unofficial periodicals, and organized women's societies across church communities.[24]

As Brigham Young and his fellows refined Joseph Smith's ideas about humanity and the sacramental rituals he introduced, Young focused increasingly on the temple endowment ceremony and the idea of "sealed" marriages, which would exist for eternity. The endowment ceremony depicted the fall of Adam and Eve and their return to God, but Young believed it also indicated how human beings would ascend to godhood themselves, inheriting the nature of their heavenly parents. Young believed that God was a man and that humanity consisted of his spirit children birthed from a heavenly mother. The growth of God's progeny increased his glory, and hence, Young taught, the ritual worship in the temple would increase the heavenly kingdoms of the man who married multiple wives. To Protestants, all this was near-blasphemous. They associated it with civilizations they believed to be degraded and backward, like the Islamic nations of the Middle East and the indigenous kingdoms of Africa, not with genuine religion. "The civilized world wonders that such a hideous caricature of

---

[24] Kathryn Daynes, *More Wives than One: The Transformation of the Mormon Marriage System, 1840–1910* (Urbana, IL: University of Illinois Press, 2001); Laurel Thatcher Ulrich, *A House Full of Females: Plural Marriage and Women's Rights in Early Mormonism* (New York: Knopf, 2017).

the Christian religion should have appeared in this most enlightened land," wrote the famous Protestant minister Josiah Strong.[25]

Indeed, many Protestants had long feared that Mormons were in the process of racial degradation. According to a number of scholars, early Mormonism upset racial categories in ways that the LDS church later grappled with.[26] Joseph Smith identified Native Americans as the descendants of the civilizations described in the Book of Mormon. He expected, then, Native Americans to respond to his preaching, and hoped many would join his new church. The Mormon settlements in Missouri existed in part to provide a base for missionary work to Native Americans, and Joseph Smith believed that the Zion built in Missouri would be a joint effort between white people and Native peoples, who had lost the true gospel and would be redeemed by the preaching of Mormon missionaries.

Smith's conversion efforts were largely unsuccessful, and he turned his attention elsewhere for the remainder of his life. In Utah, though, these dreams again revived. Brigham Young and other LDS leaders hoped that their move into the Salt Lake Valley would provide the opportunity to convert the Ute and Paiute peoples. In his early years in Utah, Young famously said he would rather feed and befriend indigenous peoples than fight them. But as with most white Christian missionary efforts, these attempts at conversion and harmonious relationships sputtered. There were some conversions; the Ute leader Walkara was baptized in 1850, and a number of other Native persons also joined the church. But such events should be viewed with caution: what white Latter-day Saints understood by conversion and baptism was not always what indigenous peoples believed these events meant. In Walkara's case, he and his people frequently traded with LDS settlers, whom he viewed as allies against other Native groups, and he likely understood his conversion as a marker of relationship rather than an intellectual assent to LDS beliefs. Later in the 1850s, tensions between LDS settlers and Walkara's people erupted into violence, and the clash's eventual resolution ended with Ute defeat and the Utah legislature authorizing settlers to indenture indigenous children, adopting them into white households as a means of assimilation and conversion. Young himself took in a young woman his family dubbed "Sally," raising her as a Latter-day Saint.[27] And he eventually pushed for a policy of Native removal and

---

[25] Strong, *Our Country*, 59.

[26] See for instance, Max Perry Mueller, *Race and the Making of the Mormon People* (Chapel Hill, NC: University of North Carolina Press, 2017) and W. Paul Reeve, *Religion of a Different Color: Race and the Mormon Struggle for Whiteness* (New York: Oxford University Press, 2014).

[27] Virginia Kerns, *Sally in Three Worlds: An Indian Captive in the House of Brigham Young* (Salt Lake City, UT: University of Utah Press, 2021).

reservations, after several more such clashes with the native people of the Salt Lake Valley.[28]

The LDS trajectory with regard to other people of color was similar. It is well established that Joseph Smith authorized the ordination of African American men to any priesthood office during his life. There are a number of well-documented African American members of the LDS church under both Joseph Smith and Brigham Young. Some, like Elijah Abel (1808–1884) and Q. Walker Lewis (1798–1856), were ordained to priesthood office and served in positions of leadership in the church. And yet, by the 1850s, Brigham Young's ideas about a racially inclusive church were changing. He was troubled by reports of interracial marriage in the church and appears to have feared the notion that such relationships would seek solemnization in the church's temples. In 1852 he delivered a speech declaring that people of African descent were descended from Cain, and that therefore they were not entitled to hold priest-hood office or participate in temple rituals.

Over several decades, Young's position was institutionalized in church pol-icy, and by the early twentieth century it was well established that Black men and women could not participate fully in the LDS church. White church leaders offered a number of racist rationales bolstering the idea beyond Young's argu-ment from genealogy, speculating that Black people possessed less righteous souls than white people did, or that in the Bible God had restricted the priest-hood to certain groups as well.[29]

By the early twentieth century, then, the LDS church had accommodated itself to the conventional racial views of most white Americans. In this way, and several others, the church was seeking to accommodate itself to American society while preserving some degree of distinctiveness.

Throughout the 1880s, the church faced mounting national criticism and even prosecution. This had begun in the 1850s, when LDS leaders publicly acknowl-edged the practice of polygamy and as rumors of what came to be called the Mountain Meadows Massacre spread. In 1857, fearing the coming of the US Army sent by President James Buchanan to install a replacement for Brigham Young as governor of the Utah territory, a group of Latter-day Saints from the southern Utah settlement of Cedar City attacked a wagon train moving through the territory, citing worry that the wagon train would carry hostile reports of the church to California. They killed more than a hundred men, women, and

---

[28] In addition to Reeve, *Religion of a Different Color* and Mueller, *Race and the Making of the Mormon People* I use on these points Amanda Hendrix-Komoto, *Imperial Zions: Religion, Race and Family in the American West* (Lincoln, NE: University of Nebraska Press, 2022).

[29] Reeve, *Religion of a Different Color*; Matthew L. Harris and Newell Bringhurst, *The Mormon Church and Blacks: A Documentary History* (Urbana, IL: University of Illinois Press, 2016).

children, and though they sought to hide their crime, it was soon uncovered. Initially LDS leaders tried to blame the massacre on the Paiute Indians, but national suspicions quickly focused on the church itself, in part because Young and other LDS leaders consistently resisted, undermined, and ignored the authority of federal officials in the territory.[30]

This national frustration with Utah's defiance of national policy was only strengthened by conflict over polygamy. In an 1878 decision, the US Supreme Court ruled that the practice of polygamy was not protected by the First Amendment's guarantees that the state would respect the free exercise of religion, on the grounds that (as Protestants assumed) the real core of religion was belief, not practice. However, church leaders urged resistance to the ruling and the laws which it upheld. By the 1880s, Congress passed a series of laws targeting polygamy and seeking to dismantle the power of the LDS church. In 1887, the Edmunds Tucker Act disincorporated the church as a legal body, authorized the federal government to take ownership of all church property, required all church members to swear oaths disavowing polygamy before they would be authorized to vote, removed the franchise from LDS women, and instituted a large fine and up to five years in prison for men who practiced polygamy.[31]

Under this pressure, in 1890 then-president of the LDS church, Wilford Woodruff (1807–1898), issued what has been called the "Manifesto" – a statement that, for the preservation of the church, urged church members to obey the law with relation to polygamy. Gradually, over the course of several decades, the practice of polygamy vanished in the LDS church. In 1904, Woodruff's successor Joseph F. Smith (1838–1918) tightened the screws. He ejected two apostles from the Quorum of the Twelve for their defiance of the Manifesto, and directed that henceforth, the practice of polygamy would be grounds for excommunication.[32]

The gradual end of plural marriage was a turning point for the LDS church. As scholars have argued, in the twentieth century the church ceased its efforts to act like a people or a nation within a nation, and instead became a religious denomination, following the rules of other American denominations. It would abide by and uphold broader American cultural standards; it would avoid overt interference in the functioning of American capitalism; it would no longer

---

[30] On national perception and rumors – some true, some untrue – about the Massacre, see Janiece Johnson, *Convicting the Mormons: The Mountain Meadows Massacre in American Culture* (Chapel Hill, NC: University of North Carolina Press, 2023).

[31] Sarah Barringer Gordon, *The Mormon Question: Polygamy and Constitutional Conflict in Nineteenth Century America* (Chapel Hill, NC: University of North Carolina Press, 2002).

[32] B. Carmon Hardy, *Solemn Covenant: The Mormon Polygamous Passage* (Urbana, IL: University of Illinois Press, 1992).

sponsor political parties. At the same time, the church did not abandon many of the religious claims that made it distinctive. It held to the notion of exclusivism, continuing to teach that it alone possessed the priestly authority to perform salvific ordinances; that its temple worship remained essential for salvation; and that its leader was God's designated prophet on the earth. In this way, as sociologist Armand Mauss has noted, the LDS church's relationship with American culture generally has oscillated, emphasizing at times distinctiveness and at other times similarity, constantly seeking both religious exclusivity but also the cultural integration necessary preserve its reputation.[33]

Pursuing both of these ideas simultaneously required the LDS church to alter its understanding of how to practice religion. Though the LDS church still sponsors strong congregations, from the early twentieth century to the present, the primary thrust of LDS teaching and practice has focused on the individual. The communal efforts of the Law of Consecration and polygamy faded, replaced by a thoroughgoing emphasis on personal moral discipline. By the 1920s, the leaders of the LDS church had made the Word of Wisdom – a guideline extrapolated from a revelation of Smith's that advised against the consumption of tea, alcohol, coffee, or tobacco – a firm boundary marker, requiring compliance for temple worship. Throughout the 1930s and 1940s, these expectations were coupled with fervent exhortations to frugality and economic responsibility as a means of coping with the Great Depression. During the sexual revolution of the 1960s, scholars have observed a rising tide of counsel in favor of sexual abstinence and traditional gender roles. The LDS church, then, became in the twentieth century a strong bureaucracy dedicated to the reformation of the individual, rather than of society.[34]

For instance, throughout the course of the twentieth century LDS leaders pursued simultaneous aims. The first was common to many American religious movements in the twentieth century, as well as the theoretical work of the scholar of religion Max Weber: rationalization, organization, and bureaucratization. Weber argued that religious institutions often endure a process of shifting from charismatic to bureaucratic authority. A long process called "correlation" – dating to the 1910s but pursued in earnest under the presidency

---

[33] Kathleen Flake, *The Politics of American Religious Identity: The Seating of Senator Reed Smoot, Mormon Apostle* (Chapel Hill, NC: University of North Carolina Press, 2005); Armand Mauss, *The Angel and the Beehive: The Mormon Struggle with Assimilation* (Urbana, IL: University of Illinois Press, 1994).

[34] Gary Shepherd and Gordon Shepherd, *A Kingdom Transformed: Early Mormonism and the Modern LDS Church* (Salt Lake City, UT: University of Utah Press, 2015); Jan Shipps, *Mormonism: The Story of a New Religious Tradition* (Urbana, IL: University of Illinois Press, 1985), 131–48.

of David O. McKay (1873–1970) in the 1960s – served to coordinate the various auxiliaries and departments that had emerged in the church since its founding.

These ranged from programs for youth and children to a Sunday school to the LDS woman's organization, the Relief Society. By the early twentieth century, each of these programs was sizable, largely independent, and modernizing in their own way. Leaders of the children's organization, Primary, were adopting modern educational theory, integrating the ideas of philosopher John Dewey to shift their focus from memorization to learning through activity and building ethics.[35] From the 1910s through the 1940s, the energetic Amy Brown Lyman, who studied at the University of Chicago, began pushing the Relief Society to embrace contemporary sociological theory about poverty. She served in positions ranging from the Relief Society's General Board to the organization's presidency, and over her long career implemented training programs in social work and modern methods of addressing social issues.[36]

Across the 1960s and 1970s, the reforms emerging from the correlation movement began to place these organizations under the authority not only of the church's president and his counselors, to whom they had long reported, but now the Quorum of the Twelve Apostles and other midlevel church leaders. Their budgets were folded into general church funds, and their programs were placed under the review of centralized committees, and the authority to write curriculum centralized as well. The church began to construct a professionalized bureaucracy, hiring managers to run these departments. Whereas once church manuals and periodicals had virtually no central institutional oversight, by the late twentieth century church printed materials were produced by a central office, usually unsigned. In 1972, the 28-story Church Office Building opened in Salt Lake City next to the temple to house this new bureaucracy.

Correlation involved other rationalizations as well. During the Great Depression, the church organized a large-scale welfare system administered by professionals, replacing the systems of relief and aid the Relief Society had long provided, but pursuing also the deeper goals of professional organization that characterized the era. In the 1950s, the church poured a large amount of resources into Brigham Young University, which began as a small teaching college in Provo, Utah, south of Salt Lake City. By the late twentieth century, BYU had emerged as a major university with tens of thousands of students.

---

[35] Carol Cornwall Madsen and Susan Staker Oman, *Sisters and Little Saints: One Hundred Years of Primary* (Salt Lake City, UT: Deseret Book, 1979), 51–2.

[36] The best work on Lyman's career is Dave Hall, *A Faded Legacy: Amy Brown Lyman and Mormon Women's Activism, 1872–1959* (Salt Lake City, UT: University of Utah Press, 2015).

While on the one hand these developments might be seen to modernize the LDS church, they should also be seen as part of a process spanning many iterations of conservative American Christianity: namely, modernization in the sense of organization and professionalization but wed also to a reemphasis of distinctiveness. Just as many conservative evangelical and Pentecostal movements adopted the latest in communications technology beginning in the early twentieth century, so too did the correlation movement serve to institutionalize conservative theology and traditional gender norms within Mormonism.

Early in the twentieth century, a number of LDS thinkers – most prominently three General Authorities named B. H. Roberts (1857–1933), John Widtsoe (1872–1952), and James Talmage (1862–1933) – wrote systematic works of theology that attempted to reconcile the ideas of Brigham Young and Joseph Smith with the ideas dominant in the United States in the Progressive Era. Primarily, this meant seeking reconciliation with contemporary science, like geology and biology, as well as social sciences. These three writers presented a Mormonism compatible with evolution, organizational theory, race science, and more, with a scientistic view of the world in which the universe was knowable through human reason. But by the mid-twentieth century, a newer generation of church leaders – primarily the apostles Joseph Fielding Smith (1876–1972, the grandson of Joseph Smith Jr.'s brother Hyrum) and Bruce R. McConkie (1915–1985) – began asserting LDS distinctiveness. They were suspicious of knowledge that emerged from outside the church and instead emphasized LDS exclusivity, arguing, as did many conservative Protestants, that most of American society was immoral, that human beings were vulnerable to sin and error, and that divine revelation was the chief source of truth. They argued for a high view of LDS authority, maintaining that the General Authorities of the LDS church were prophets just as Joseph Smith was, and that their statements should be regarded as the will of God. Because their ideas were ascendant in the LDS church during the era of correlation, it was their theology of science, salvation, and denominationalism that prevailed in the LDS church by the end of the twentieth century.[37]

Like many conservative Protestants in the United States, the LDS church leadership also began to perceive the changes in twentieth-century gender norms as a threat. Though the church had abandoned polygamy, it retained the

---

[37] On correlation and its cultural impact, see Mauss, *The Angel and the Beehive*; Matthew Bowman, *The Mormon People: The Making of an American Faith* (New York: Random House, 2012); and Gregory Prince and William Robert Wright, *David O. McKay and the Rise of Modern Mormonism* (Salt Lake City, UT: University of Utah Press, 2005).

ritual of sealing and through the twentieth century wedded it to monogamous heterosexual marriage and to a vision of God as a male deity, who, literally with a heavenly mother, was the father of the human soul. The sealing ritual, now understood to bind earthly marriages together for eternity and to the family of God, was an imitation of this heavenly marriage. Many Latter-day Saints thus perceived the changing gender politics of the 1960s and 1970s as a threat. The emerging feminist movement and the sexual revolution threatened this vision of what divinity looked like, and church leaders reacted in kind. Many began to teach gender complementarianism and essentialism, arguing that God intended fathers to preside in the home and to provide for their families, while mothers were intended to raise children and nurture families. The LDS church lent political muscle to the 1970s defeat of the Equal Rights Amendment, which would have barred legal distinctions between men and women in the United States, and moved to marginalize and sometimes excommunicate church members who participated in activism, like the prominent advocate for the Equal Rights Amendment Sonia Johnson. By the 1990s, most Latter-day Saints in the United States identified with social conservatism and the Religious Right.[38]

While the church's firm complementarianism began to dwindle in the twenty-first century – as rhetoric about separate spheres in church venues and policies on birth control began to shift to accommodate two-income households and women with careers – through the early twenty-first century the Church shifted its focus to concern about same-sex marriage, also seen as a threat to the divine model of heterosexual marriage. As with many conservative Christian groups, for much of the twentieth century LDS leaders spoke of homosexuality as a psychological disorder and perhaps a sin. By the early twenty-first century, that language had faded in favor of rhetoric based on the notion of "same-sex attraction," a term church leaders used to describe homosexuality as a regrettable burden to bear, but not sinful in and of itself. True to these ideas, from the 1980s through 2008 LDS leaders lent weight and support to various state political campaigns seeking to prevent same-sex marriages. In such a campaign in 2008 in California, the church attracted negative publicity surprising to its leaders. Following the Supreme Court's 2014 decision ruling same-sex marriage constitutional, they shifted strategy toward seeking to promote anti-discrimination laws for LGBT Americans while also allowing the church itself to maintain expectations for heterosexual

---

[38] Colleen McDannell, *Sister Saints: Mormon Women since the End of Polygamy* (New York: Oxford University Press, 2018); Martha Sonntag Bradley, *Pedestals and Podiums: Utah Women, Religious Authority, and Equal Rights* (Salt Lake City, UT: Signature Books, 2005).

marriage, and to enforce such expectations within church institutions like Brigham Young University.[39]

The LDS church enjoyed explosive growth in the second half of the twentieth century. From a church with under a million members at the end of World War II, by the year 2000 the church had reached ten million members by the year 2000, with a majority living outside the United States. This tracked the growth of Christianity generally. In the LDS church as in Roman Catholicism or many Protestant denominations, growth in those years slowed in the United States and Europe but expanded rapidly in Latin America and Africa. People in these places had long been familiar with colonial Christianity, but in the age of decolonization many found appealing the opportunity to make an American faith their own.

A number of scholars have written on the reasons for LDS growth in the Global South. Among the innovations of the correlation program was a strong, well-organized missionary program. Since the 1950s the church has exerted much pressure upon every young man (and left the option open for young women) to serve a mission in their late teens and early twenties. Missionaries are provided with an extensive support structure and rigorous, standardized curriculum. But in addition, scholars have noted that the church's emphasis on modern prophecy, new scripture, and ritual worship is appealing in the Global South. Throughout the twentieth century, the LDS church began building temples around the world at a rapid pace and encouraged members to participate in the endowment ceremony regularly – if not for themselves, then by proxy for the dead. This connection to ancestors is particularly appealing in Africa and Latin America as well.[40]

However real this appeal might be, the church also faces significant obstacles in its international growth. While the church successfully baptizes many in these regions, many of these converts do not remain active participants in the church for an extensive period of time. Thus, though the LDS church in the early twenty-first century claimed a majority of its membership outside the United States, it is highly likely that a majority of its participants remain American.[41] Many scholars have ascribed this phenomenon to the success of the correlation

---

[39] Taylor Petrey, *Tabernacles of Clay: Gender and Sexuality in Modern Mormonism* (Chapel Hill, NC: University of North Carolina Press, 2020).

[40] Philip Jenkins, "Letting Go: Exploring Mormon Growth in Africa," *Journal of Mormon History* 35:2 (Spring 2009), 1–25; D. D. Hurlbut, "The LDS Church and the Problem of Race: Mormonism in Nigeria, 1946–1978," *International Journal of African Historical Studies* 51:1 (2018): 1–16.

[41] Claudia Bushman, *Contemporary Mormonism: Latter-day Saints in Modern America* (Westport, CT: Greenwood Press, 2006), 57–75; David G. Stewart, "The Dynamics of LDS Growth in the Twenty-First Century," in R. Gordon Shepherd, A. Gary Shepherd, and Ryan Cragun, eds., *The Palgrave Handbook of Global Mormonism* (London: Palgrave Macmillan, 2020), 163–205.

movement. Correlation regulated worship, music, and dress as much as it did theology, and it institutionalized white American norms in all of these ways as much as it enshrined conservative theology.[42]

Two examples demonstrate how these issues caused turbulence in the twentieth-century global church. In Mexico in the 1930s, a large number of indigenous Mexicans formed what they called "the Church of Jesus Christ of Latter-day Saints – Third Convention" in response to a lack of attention paid to a number of missives they had sent to Salt Lake City calling for materials in Spanish and more native leadership in the Mexican church. While acknowledging the authority of the General Authorities, Third Convention leaders taught that the Book of Mormon indicated that the indigenous peoples of the Americas had a special role to play in the church that the white American leadership had ignored. For years, American church leaders in Salt Lake City discounted these complaints and branded the ideas behind the Third Convention as heretical. The theologian Margarito Bautista was excommunicated from the church and organized his own branch of Mormonism that embraced indigeneity.[43]

In West Africa in the 1950s and 1960s, issues of culture and race similarly thwarted LDS growth. In the 1950s local Africans discovered LDS materials and began to practice a version of African Mormonism using the Book of Mormon. The LDS church was both unwilling and unable to send leaders to Africa because its ban on Black participation in the priesthood meant that newly independent West African governments in Nigeria and Ghana, particularly, were unwilling to allow LDS missionaries. At the same time, Africans continued to develop a form of Mormonism on their own, one far more charismatic and improvisational than LDS officials were comfortable with. When LDS missionaries from the United States arrived in Africa in the late 1970s, they moved quickly to eliminate practices like prophecy, glossolalia, and emotional worship.[44]

By 1978, the church's ban on full participation of Black members was attracting a great deal of criticism while also causing strain within the church.

---

[42] For arguments to this end, see Jenkins, "Letting Go"; Laurie Maffly-Kipp, "Pulling Toward Zion: Mormonism in Its Global Dimensions," in Shepherd, Shepherd, and Cragun, eds., *The Palgrave Handbook of Global Mormonism,* 143–163; Hazel O'Brien, *Irish Mormons: Reconciling Identity in Global Mormonism* (Urbana, IL: University of Illinois Press, 2023), 60–2.

[43] Elisa Eastwood Pulido, *The Spiritual Evolution of Margarito Bautista: Mexican Mormon Evangelizer, Polygamist Dissident, and Utopian Founder, 1878–1961* (New York: Oxford University Press, 2019), 159–82.

[44] David Dmitri Hurlbut, *Nigerian Converts, Mormon Missionaries, and the Priesthood Revelation: Mormonism in Nigeria, 1946–1978* (Boston, MA: Boston University Working Papers in African Studies, 2015); Russell Stevenson, "We Have Prophetesses: Mormonism in Ghana, 1964–1979," *Journal of Mormon History* 41:3 (2015), 221–37.

By the early 1970s LDS missionaries were having success in Brazil, but widespread African ancestry among Brazilians made it difficult for church leaders to regularly enforce the ban. Similarly, in the United States, after more than two decades of the Black freedom movement, the ban seemed increasingly anachronistic and routinely drew attacks in the press. After much pondering, in 1978 church president Spencer W. Kimball (1895–1985) declared that a revelation had inspired him to announce a new policy: access to the priesthood and temple worship should no longer be restricted on account of race.[45]

Between the end of the restriction and the beginning of the twenty-first century, the LDS church grew quite rapidly. Its membership passed ten million by the year 2000, a tenfold increase over the previous fifty years alone. Most of that growth was in the Global South, as membership grew far more rapidly outside the United States, However, other indicators of growth – the organization of units of the church like wards and stakes, for instance – indicated that raw membership numbers do not give an accurate indication of participation in the church. In the first decades of the twenty-first century, church leaders tightened requirements for convert baptism, hoping to allow only those committed to participation to join the church. Growth consequently slowed, but indications show that participation in the church outside the United States still lags behind the participation of North Americans.[46]

Inside the United States, LDS church growth has slowed as well. The church attracted increased publicity in the early twenty-first century, a period sometimes referred to as "the Mormon moment." That moment was variously dated to the 2002 Winter Olympics in Salt Lake City, a wave of depictions of the church in popular media like a Broadway show and several movies, and, most famously, to former Massachusetts governor Mitt Romney's two bids for the Republican presidential nomination – one failed in 2008 and one successful four years later.

While during the mid twentieth century the LDS church was often praised for its adherence to the Word of Wisdom, the self-reliance its welfare plan promoted, and its embrace of traditional gender politics, by the early twenty-first century, changing cultural norms meant the church attracted criticism for many of those same positions and policies.[47] Some scholars have described this renewed tension as reminiscent of the church's earlier periods of resistance to

---

[45] J. B. Haws, *The Mormon Image in the American Mind: Fifty Years of Public Perception* (New York: Oxford University Press, 2014), 47–74; Edward Kimball, "Spencer Kimball and the Revelation on Priesthood," *BYU Studies* 47:2 (2008), 4–78.

[46] Samuel M. Otterstrom and B. M. Plewe, "Geographical Diffusion and Growth Patterns of the Church of Jesus Christ of Latter-day Saints since World War II," in Shepherd, Shepherd, and Cragun, eds., *The Palgrave Handbook of Global Mormonism,* 91–141.

[47] Haws, *The Mormon Image in the American Mind,* 236–81.

assimilation to American culture. For them, it may explain, at least in part why, like many other religious denominations, the church struggled to retain its younger members by the 2010s.[48]

Community of Christ

Both the Reorganized Church of Jesus Christ of Latter Day Saints (RLDS, today Community of Christ) and the Fundamentalist Church of Jesus Christ of Latter-day Saints (FLDS) fashioned themselves to some extent in opposition to the LDS church. Each perceived the LDS church's means of balance between the distinctiveness of its own identity and assimilation with the society around it to be inadequate in some way. For the first founders of the RLDS church, the LDS church's devotion to practices like polygamy and temple worship seemed unappealing ad even disreputable.[49]

The Reorganized Church of Jesus Christ of Latter Day Saints was formally organized in 1860 as the "Church of Jesus Christ of Latter Day Saints," adding the word "Reorganized" in 1872 to emphasize its distinctiveness from the LDS church. In 2001, the church took on the name Community of Christ – not merely to distinguish itself from the LDS church, but also to emphasize an ecumenical Christian identity that was increasingly important to the RLDS church by the mid-twentieth century.

For those who organized the RLDS church (as I will call it while discussing its history before 2001), the fragmentation following the death of Joseph Smith Jr. was telling and inevitable. They did not recognize the authority of the Quorum of the Twelve Apostles to take the leadership of the church and believed that figures like James Strang and Sidney Rigdon only contributed to a period of disorganization and tumult in the religious community Joseph Smith had founded. Many of them believed that Joseph Smith had designated his son, Joseph Smith III (1832–1914), to follow him, pointing to a number of revelations that implied a lineal aspect to priesthood authority. Similarly, there existed an oral and familial tradition that Joseph Smith Jr. had given his son a blessing in 1839 that conferred the right to lead the church. Emma Smith, Lucy Mack Smith, and other members of the Smith family believed that leadership should pass in this way, and all the Smiths but the family of Hyrum Smith (1800–1844), killed alongside Joseph Smith, declined to accompany Brigham Young to Utah.[50]

---

[48] Jana Riess, *The Next Mormons: How Millennials Are Changing the LDS Church* (New York: Oxford University Press, 2019).

[49] Again, this argument draws on Duffy and Howlett, *Mormonism*.

[50] On the chaos of succession and the tradition of the 1839 blessing, see D. Michael Quinn, *The Mormon Hierarchy: Origins of Power* (Salt Lake City, UT: Signature Books, 1994), 187–245.

Joseph Smith III was eleven years old when his father died, but by his early twenties, a number of Mormons – many who had once followed James Strang, or others who had never accepted the authority of Brigham Young – were approaching him asking him to take the leadership of a reorganized church. Smith III declined until 1860, when, after a period of great personal tumult and growing moral seriousness, he announced that he had received a revelation from God that a reorganization would be appropriate. In April of 1860 he attended a gathering of scattered Mormons in Amboy, Illinois, and announced the reorganization of the Church of Jesus Christ of Latter Day Saints. Smith III announced that he accepted the authority of the Bible, the Book of Mormon, and the "book of covenants," a collection of his father's revelations, but rejected Brigham Young's claim to authority and, particularly, the LDS practice of polygamy. Indeed, the RLDS church has increased emphasis on the Bible since the 1960s though it uses the "Inspired Version" based on Joseph Smith's reworking of the text, and accepts and has continued to add to the collection of revelations called the Doctrine and Covenants.[51]

The early years of Smith III's leadership focused on gathering in many scattered Mormons. Initially this meant reconstructing a bureaucratic and priestly leadership. As did Brigham Young, Smith III followed the organizational patterns his father had laid down. RLDS church leadership consisted of a presidency of three, a president and two counselors, and a quorum of twelve apostles, which Smith III viewed primarily as missionaries – their function in Joseph Smith's church – rather than as chief administrators, as they had become in the LDS church. He also organized a "high council," a group of advisors that had existed under Joseph Smith but had become primarily a local authority in the LDS church. The reconstitution of all of these offices was gradual, taking Smith III until 1873, when he declared that revelation had given him the authority and the direction to do it in totality.

Constructing such a bureaucratic hierarchy required, of course, a population of church members sizable enough to provide candidates and to be governed. Much of what remained of Smith's time in the 1860s and 1870s was taken up with mission work and determining the nature of RLDS identity. He created a publishing house that could spread the RLDS message, organized missions, and warily endorsed eager members of his reorganized church who came to him with a proposal to build a Zion community.

Smith III was hesitant about the idea when it was first proposed to him in the early 1860s, having a vivid memory of the suspicions such gatherings had aroused among his father's neighbors in Illinois and Missouri. He urged

---

[51] Roger Launius, *Joseph Smith III: Pragmatic Prophet* (Urbana, IL: University of Illinois, 1988).

caution, but eventually approved communal experiments, first in Nauvoo, Illinois, then – acknowledging that Nauvoo's rural location made it particularly difficult to communicate effectively with a church flung across the Midwest – Lamoni, Iowa, founded by an RLDS economic commune called the Order of Enoch. The town became headquarters of the RLDS church in 1881. Thirteen years later, Smith III founded Graceland College, an RLDS-sponsored college, in Lamoni. When a number of RLDS members began to flock to Independence, Missouri, Joseph Smith Jr.'s dreamed site of Zion, Joseph Smith III himself moved there in the last years before his death in 1914.[52]

The work of reorganization included a number of missions to Utah, a task Smith III entrusted in part to his brothers, the younger sons of Joseph Smith Jr. By the 1860s there was a small branch of the RLDS church in Salt Lake City, and in the later part of that decade and the early 1870s, several Smiths, including Smith III, visited multiple times. Despite several publicized clashes with the LDS hierarchy, including somewhat tense meetings with Brigham Young and Joseph Smith III's cousin Joseph F. Smith (1838–1918), by then an LDS apostle, few converts were made. When Brigham Young died in 1877, some urged Joseph Smith III to seek the presidency of the LDS church, but he demurred. By that point, the two churches were engaged in a legal battle over ownership of the Kirtland Temple, which Joseph Smith Jr. had built and dedicated in the 1830s. The court eventually ruled that the RLDS church was the legal heir to Joseph Smith Jr.'s church, and thus Smith III eventually gained possession of the temple.[53]

This conflict was important to the RLDS church, because Joseph Smith III and his brothers believed that the LDS church had materially departed from Joseph Smith Jr.'s legacy in numerous ways and that, therefore, their own church was the genuine version of Mormonism. In many cases the things Smith III rejected had indeed originated with Joseph Smith Jr., but his son, who was only a boy when the founding prophet died, lacked familiarity with them, and his mother Emma, Smith III's most direct connection to his father, restrained her son's efforts. The most significant of these issues was polygamy. It appears that Emma Smith assured her children that their father had never practiced polygamy, and Smith III and his brothers believed that the practice originated with Brigham Young; this was part of the argument they mounted to regain control of the Kirtland Temple.[54]

---

[52] Launius, *Joseph Smith III*, 174–85.

[53] David Howlett, *Kirtland Temple: A Biography of a Shared Sacred Space* (Urbana, IL: University of Illinois, 2014).

[54] On Emma Smith's relationship with Joseph III and polygamy see Valeen Tippetts Avery and Linda King Newell, *Mormon Enigma: Emma Hale Smith* (Urbana, IL: University of Illinois Press, 1984), 278–80.

The practices the leaders of the LDS church accentuated and the RLDS dismissed or downplayed were, like polygamy, generally those which distinguished the former from the Protestant majority in the United States. Joseph Smith III's version of Mormonism affirmed the distinctiveness of his father's revelations and the authoritative power of its priesthood, but he dismissed his father's late-in-life ideas about a corporeal God whose divinity human beings could aspire to. He was uninterested in temple rituals like the endowment and the sealing of marriages, or the sacred undergarments Latter-day Saints wore after participating in the endowment. And just as the LDS church leadership began to emphasize the importance of the Word of Wisdom, Joseph Smith III counseled not abstinence but temperance, and did not make the revelation a boundary marker for his faith, as the LDS church did. In sum, then, Joseph Smith III's version of Mormonism sought to find accommodation with the mainstream of American life. While the LDS church was forced into a similar stance and later embraced much of it, it also held Protestant culture at arm's length. The RLDS church increasingly pursued reconciliation, seeking, by the late twentieth century, to find a space for Mormonism within the ecumenical consensus of mainline Protestantism.[55]

Joseph Smith III died in 1914, after fifty-four years of service, and he left a strong, well-organized denomination headquartered in Lamoni, Iowa. His son, Frederick Madison Smith (1874–1946), succeeded him the next year, at age forty-one. His accession to the presidency was uncontroversial; Smith III believed in the doctrine of lineal succession but also that God had confirmed Frederick was the right person for the job. In a mark of the diverging ideas of authority in the two churches, Smith III issued a letter of instruction two years before his death stating his wish that lineal succession be implemented; the Quorum of the Twelve Apostles and other general authorities in the RLDS acknowledged the counsel but refused to be bound by it. Nonetheless, they accepted Frederick M. Smith (often known as Fred) anyway.[56]

Fred M. Smith was in his person a symbol of RLDS assimilation to the norms of broader American Protestant culture. He held a PhD in psychology from Clark University, where he studied under G. Stanley Hall (1844–1924), one of the leading American psychologists of his generation and an advocate for what was then broadly called "progressivism," the idea that expertise and social science would aid Americans in more properly organizing their society. As laws were passed, agencies established, and experts placed at their head, progressives believed, the ills of human society could be ameliorated. Hall

---

[55] This claim echoes Howlett, in *Kirtland Temple,* 1.

[56] Paul Edwards, *The Chief: An Administrative Biography of Fred M. Smith* (Independence, MO: Herald House, 1988), 45–8.

believed that psychology was an invaluable tool in confronting challenges from education to crime, and his student, Fred M. Smith, imbibed this confidence. Smith's dissertation argued that religion was a mode of channeling deep mystical energies through the person, which might be directed in ecstatic experience or – Smith's preference – toward greater self-discipline and moral reform. He found inspiration in the social gospel movement, an alliance of progressive Christians who sought to remake American society in ethical and humane ways, curbing industrial abuses and promoting both individual and social morality. When Frederick ascended to the presidency of the RLDS church, he sought to bend the institution in these directions.[57]

Fred M. Smith's tenure at the head of the RLDS church lasted until 1946, and he left a permanent mark on the institution. After his death, he was succeeded first by his brother Israel (1876–1958) and then his brother Wallace (1900–1989); between them the three sons of Joseph Smith III headed the church until 1978. They also presided, and to some extent directed, their church's pursuit of religious modernism. As defined by William Hutchison, its preeminent scholar, the modernist movement in American religion was committed to the adaptation of religious belief and practice to changing culture, and the faith that God's will could be revealed in broader cultural change, not simply direct revelation. Modernists tended toward optimism, hope, and the faith that a religious tradition could find inspiration and direction within the society and culture that surrounded it.[58]

The century following the death of Joseph Smith III saw dramatic progress toward modernism in the RLDS church, culminating in its adoption of the name Community of Christ in 2001. But these developments did not come easily. The sons of Smith III confronted resistance as they sought to push their church in new directions. The first ten years of Frederick's presidency saw a prolonged struggle for authority with an older generation of leaders – apostles and other authorities called by Joseph Smith III who were suspicious of the young president's ambitions. By the 1920s, Frederick had succeeded in establishing what he called "supreme directional control," centralizing financial and decision-making power in the church in his own presidency. He then launched what he called a "stewardship" program that attempted to build a series of communal settlements, rationally organized and made up of individuals of demonstrated moral discipline, whom he hoped would build a model Zion community.

---

[57] Larry Hunt, "Frederick Madison Smith: The Formative Years of an RLDS President," *Journal of Mormon History* 4 (1977), 67–89. See more broadly Larry E. Hunt, *F. M Smith: Saint as Reformer* (Independence, MO: Herald House, 1982).

[58] William R. Hutchison, *The Modernist Impulse in American Protestantism* (Cambridge, MA: Harvard University Press, 1992), 4–8.

Though it collapsed under the weight of the Great Depression, this effort at social reform left the RLDS church with a vision of Zion as less a specific place than a communal effort at economic and social rebuilding. It also made training and education key values for the pastoral leadership of the RLDS.[59]

Under the leadership of Frederick M. Smith's brothers, this modernist impulse toward a religion emphasizing social justice, rational order, and engagement with modern culture found an ally in what scholars have described as the ecumenical movement. This group of Protestants, most belonging to what came to be called the mainline denominations after World War II, consciously downplayed theological difference and hoped to mobilize organizations, churchly and otherwise, against broad social evils, like poverty and war. They organized large-scale ecumenical alliances, most prominently the National Council of Churches, and began to reconsider traditional Christian aims like mission work as opportunities to celebrate cultural pluralism and alleviate suffering rather than to pursue simple denominational growth. In 1966, RLDS President W. Wallace Smith issued a declaration, "The Church and the Social Order," which echoed many of these principles and placed the RLDS church behind them.[60]

Through the 1950s and 1960s, key leaders of the RLDS church attended Protestant seminaries and were educated in the ecumenical impulse. For instance, Roy Cheville (1897–1986) was educated at the University of Chicago Divinity School, a center of modernist thought. He served as pastor of the RLDS church's Graceland University for decades in the mid-twentieth century and took office as the church's presiding patriarch in 1958. From both positions he wrote dozens of works promoting ecumenism. By 1960, the church began issuing curriculum written from the ecumenical point of view. Similarly, other RLDS leaders began pursuing international missions in the 1960s, and, like the apostle Charles Neff (1922–1991), were greatly influenced by the international work of ecumenical organizations and began pushing the RLDS leadership to rethink what mission work could or should be. In 1967, the twenty or so highest leaders of the RLDS church held a series of sessions with a pair of Methodist theologians and, under their ecumenical influence, began a reframing of what the RLDS church understood its identity to be. Scholar Roger Launius identifies the 1960s as the decade in which the RLDS church abandoned its identity as a "sect" – a religious group self-consciously set apart from others and

---

[59] David Howlett, "The Death and Resurrection of the RLDS Zion: A Case Study in 'Failed Prophecy,' 1930–70," *Dialogue: A Journal of Mormon Thought* 40:3 (2007), 112–31.

[60] The most able chronicler of this impulse is David Hollinger, *Christianity's American Fate: How Religion Became More Conservative and Society More Secular* (Princeton, NJ: Princeton University Press, 2022).

maintaining a claim to exclusive truth and knowledge – and instead became a "denomination," understanding itself as one expression of a broader ecumenical Christianity.[61]

These theological shifts were paralleled with organizational development. No standardization process like correlation occurred in the RLDS church; thus, by the end of the twentieth century, variances in worship and organization were not uncommon. Some congregations had adopted liturgical forms from Protestant churches, such as the offertory, a collection of donations during worship. The office of bishop, which in Joseph Smith's lifetime was responsible for finances, had by the mid-nineteenth century evolved in the LDS church to refer to the leader of a congregation. But in the RLDS church, bishops remained financial officers, while the leaders of local congregations were by the end of the nineteenth century referred to as pastors or presiding elders. By the late twentieth century, and in contrast to the LDS, some congregations paid their pastors, especially as many began to attend Protestant seminaries.

The trend toward modernism did not come without controversy – perhaps most dramatically when Wallace B. Smith, president of the RLDS church from 1978 to 1995, made a series of announcements that broke with long-standing RLDS tradition. In 1984 Wallace Smith announced a revelation that directed that women would henceforth be ordained to priesthood office. He also stated that it was time to build the temple in Independence, Missouri, that Joseph Smith Jr. had foreseen a century and a half before. This was controversial because the temple was not built on the land Joseph Smith Jr. had originally identified, and because critics were skeptical of Wallace Smith's declaration that the temple would be a monument to international and personal peace – something that seemed distressingly ecumenical and not distinctively Christian. Finally, in 1995 Wallace Smith broke a final tradition, announcing that he would retire as president of the RLDS church, to be succeeded by W. Grant MacMurray (b. 1947) – the first RLDS president who was not a Smith. One of MacMurray's early actions was shepherding the renaming of the RLDS church to "Community of Christ," a name chosen precisely because it would reorient the faith away from its seemingly sectarian roots and toward a broader ecumenical Christianity.[62]

---

[61] Roger Launius, "Coming of Age: The Reorganized Church of Jesus Christ of Latter Day Saints in the 1960s," *Dialogue: A Journal of Mormon Thought* 28:2 (1995), 31–57.

[62] See the discussion in Craig Campbell, *Images of the New Jerusalem: Latter Day Saint Faction Interpretations of Independence, Missouri* (Knoxville, TN: University of Tennessee Press, 2004), 232–4.

Over the previous forty years there had been a trickle of discontent among many more traditional members of the RLDS church, some bristling as the ecumenical church leadership began downplaying the distinctiveness of Joseph Smith's restoration or casting doubt on the historicity of the Book of Mormon. For instance, in 1966, several RLDS members founded a group called Foundation for Research on Ancient America, designed to defend the historicity of the Book of Mormon against what they perceived to be neglect from the church's leadership.[63] Such dissent came to full flower upon Wallace Smith's announcement that the priesthood would be opened to men and women alike. Several branches of the RLDS church across the country began to protest, and perhaps 25,000 members separated themselves from RLDS leadership. In April 2000, under the leadership of Frederick Larsen (1932–2019), the grandson of Frederick Madison Smith, some such branches organized the Remnant Church of Jesus Christ of Latter Day Saints. For the Remnant Church, the Reorganization was the genuine church restored by Joseph Smith Jr., until it drifted off course into the ecumenical movement.[64]

But despite such protests, RLDS and later Community of Christ leaders pointed to their heritage, noting their tradition's long commitment to social justice and the notion of Zion as a place without poverty or suffering. They noted, for instance, that Joseph Smith III had long been an advocate for racial equality, ordaining Black men to the priesthood at the same time that the LDS church was formulating a policy against it. They maintained also that Joseph Smith Jr. understood restoration as a long, evolving process, and that he spoke of revelation as an ongoing practice that will change as history itself develops. To Community of Christ leaders, the heritage of Joseph Smith's restoration is the pursuit of truth, the defiance of traditional institutions, and a willingness to seek social justice.

Mormon Fundamentalism

In the first week of October in 1890, newspapers in Salt Lake City carried the announcement that Wilford Woodruff, president of the LDS church, had issued the Manifesto. Woodruff's statement declared his intention to henceforth abide by federal laws regarding polygamy. He also urged other members of the church to do the same. This caused an uproar. Many members of the LDS church were confused at so sudden a reversal of the practice they had been intent on defending against all opposition for decades. Moreover, they were puzzled

---

[63] See for instance William Russell, "Defenders of the Faith: Varieties of RLDS Dissent," *Sunstone* 14:3 (1990), 14–19.

[64] Campbell, *Images of the New Jerusalem,* 283–6.

that the Manifesto contained little in the way of practical guidance. For instance, it was unclear whether polygamist church members should treat all marriages beyond a man and woman's first null and void, or simply from that point on enter into no new such marriages; it was unclear whether the Manifesto applied only within the United States; it was unclear whether or how it might be enforced.[65]

There was disagreement. Some men believed it required them to abandon polygamous spouses; others remained in polygamous relationships but pursued no more. Still others continued to marry polygamously in Mexico, in Canada, or in secret in the United States. Woodruff lived for eight more years, and over that span grew increasingly insistent that the Manifesto was not simply a stopgap political contingency, but rather inspired. Woodruff said that God had assured him that the step was essential for the temporal preservation of the LDS church. Indeed, Congress had authorized the federal government to seize the church's assets, and the courts did not seem inclined to stop this from happening. Woodruff believed that the church was in peril, and over the remaining years of his presidency, he saw the president of the United States pardon Mormon men for their violations of the law, and Congress, satisfied that LDS polygamy was over, authorize Utah to enter the United States as the forty-fifth state. He went to his grave certain that the Manifesto had saved his church.[66]

And yet, there remained a strong cohort of members of his church who insisted the Manifesto was merely for show. Historians have documented that the General Authorities of the church, including Woodruff himself, authorized dozens of plural marriages for more than a decade after the Manifesto. Though the number of plural marriages indeed plummeted after 1890, they did not vanish entirely. Many Latter-day Saints believed that church settlements in Mexico and Canada, which were founded in the 1880s as a haven from US prosecution of polygamy, were safe places for polygamous marriages. In the Mexican Mormon settlements, where several thousand church members lived by the end of the 1800s, a handful of members of the Quorum of the Twelve Apostles regularly performed plural marriages. Similarly, other local leaders of the church – officiants in temple sealings, for instance – sometimes performed plural marriages without authorization. When apostles or local leaders performed such marriages in the United States, a variety of legal trickeries were

---

[65] See, for instance, the incredulous response of Church official and apologist B. H. Roberts in John Sillito, *History's Apprentice: The Diary of B. H. Roberts, 1890–1898* (Salt Lake City, UT: Signature Books, 2004), 222–5.

[66] This process is best covered in Hardy, *Solemn Covenant* and Gordon, *The Mormon Question*. See also Gustive O. Larson, *The Americanization of Utah for Statehood* (San Marino, CA: Huntington Library, 1971).

used to evade the law: men would divorce a first wife but continue cohabitation before marrying a second, use a pseudonym to marry, and so forth.[67]

By the early twentieth century, wary journalists and members of Congress learned that polygamy remained in the hidden nooks and crannies of the LDS church, and public pressure was again brought to bear. When the Utah legislature elected LDS apostle and monogamist Reed Smoot (1862–1941) to the United States Senate in 1902, the unlucky senator-elect underwent months of hearings in which senators grilled him and a number of LDS leaders on the topic of the church's loyalty to the United States. Smoot was eventually seated, but the ordeal persuaded church president Joseph F. Smith to take action. In April 1904, Smith announced to the church's General Conference that church leaders would now punish new polygamous marriages with excommunication from the church – a statement sometimes called the "Second Manifesto."[68]

And such discipline happened. In 1905 Smith forced two apostles, Matthias Cowley (1858–1940) and John W. Taylor (1858–1916), out of the Quorum of the Twelve for their refusal to accept the Second Manifesto. Taylor was later excommunicated and Cowley disfellowshipped, an act that restricted Cowley's membership but stopped short of cutting him off entirely. Smith directed the remaining apostles to investigate continued polygamy and begin excommunications when warranted. He directed local leaders to take action when they became aware of new polygamous marriages, and many were severed from the church.

It was in this atmosphere that the movement that has come to be called Mormon fundamentalism was born. There is no single church or denomination that can be called Mormon fundamentalism. Rather, there are a collection of groups. The largest of these are the Fundamentalist Church of Jesus Christ of Latter Day Saints and the Apostolic United Brethren; each claims thousands of members, although the FLDS church lost a great number of members in the early twenty-first century after a series of scandals. Others claim only a few hundred or few dozen. In addition, there are likely thousands of independent Mormon fundamentalists who identify with the movement but belong to no organization.

Fundamentalism emerged from two sources. One was simple dissent and discontent with the ever-intensifying pressure within the LDS church to end the practice of plural marriage on the part of a number of local members of that church. They felt that the General Authorities had for years been secretly encouraging polygamy and believed that the practice was commanded by God

---

[67] D. Michael Quinn, "LDS Church Authority and New Plural Marriages, 1890–1904," *Dialogue: A Journal of Mormon Thought* 18:1 (1985), 9–105.

[68] Flake, *Politics of American Religious Identity*.

and should not be ended simply because of legal pressure. Among these, and representative of them, was a man named Joseph Musser (1872–1954), an official in a stake of the church in the southern Salt Lake Valley. Musser knew that many leaders of the church had solemnized polygamous marriages after the Manifesto and did not see why the Second Manifesto should be any different. Several times in the 1900s and 1910s he was called in to meet with apostles of the church; several times he told them frankly that he still believed that polygamy was commanded by God and thus would continue telling others that it was. After nearly fifteen years of such interviews, he was excommunicated in 1921, when apostles learned of his plans to marry a fourth wife.[69]

Beyond such local resistance, the other impetus for Mormon fundamentalism came from a man named Lorin Woolley (1856–1934). Woolley grew up just north of Salt Lake City. He was a young man in the 1880s, when his father had at times hid church president John Taylor (in office 1879–1887) from federal agents seeking to arrest him for practicing polygamy. By the time of the Second Manifesto, Woolley was a middle-aged man and something of an eccentric; he sometimes claimed to have been a Secret Service agent and to have converted multiple US presidents in secret to Mormonism. But his most consequential claim would prove to be foundational to the Mormon fundamentalist movement. In 1912, Woolley published a pamphlet stating that while John Taylor was secreted in the Woolley home in 1886, Taylor received a revelation declaring polygamy to be "everlasting," and specifically denying the possibility that God would allow it to end. This claim was startling enough and has since been somewhat validated: photographs of such a document in Taylor's handwriting exist and appear to be genuine. But beyond this, Woolley claimed that the day the revelation was received, Taylor was visited by Jesus Christ and a resurrected Joseph Smith, and under their direction formed a new priestly order, a seven-man Priesthood Council or Council of Friends including both Woolleys, father and son, and charged with preserving the practice of polygamy on the earth independent of what the LDS church might do.[70]

Woolley's story was galvanizing. Previously, dissidents like Musser or John W. Taylor had nowhere to go but to excommunication. Now, though, Woolley offered them something new – a priesthood hierarchy of their own; a history; a theory; a community. The three primary branches of Mormonism – LDS,

---

[69] Cristina Rosetti, *Joseph White Musser: A Mormon Fundamentalist* (Urbana, IL: University of Illinois, 2024).

[70] On Woolley, see Brian C. Hales, *Modern Polygamy and Mormon Fundamentalism: The Generations after the Manifesto* (Salt Lake City, UT: Greg Kofford Books, 2006); and Martha Sonntag Bradley, *Kidnapped from that Land: The Government Raids on the Short Creek Polygamists* (Salt Lake City, UT: University of Utah Press, 1993).

RLDS, and fundamentalist – divided over the practice of polygamy, among other things, but each also rested its claim to authority not simply upon that dispute, but on other sources as well. Like the Mormon movement in total, generated from the charismatic authority of Joseph Smith and sustained by his construction of an organization, each branch of the movement could point to a central leader – Brigham Young, Joseph Smith III, Lorin Woolley – who offered a charismatic claim to authority but built from it a stable institutional structure. Young moved the allegiance of his followers to the Quorum of the Twelve Apostles; Joseph Smith III directed the authority that only the son of Joseph Smith Jr. might invoke into the construction of a new church; Lorin Woolley not only claimed special authority from John Taylor, but also provided the grounds for the creation of a new priestly council. It was the beginning of a new branch of Mormonism.

But while the RLDS church and eventually the LDS church sought some degree of accommodation with the world around them, taking measures necessary to ensure that they would thrive, or at least exist in peace, in a largely Protestant society, Woolley and his followers perceived such measures as compromise and dilution. This is not to say, though, that Mormon fundamentalism simply preserved unaltered the Mormonism of Joseph Smith. Though fundamentalism as a broader concept seeks to claim the charismatic authority that a pristine connection to the past might offer, it does not simply replicate that past. It cannot. Rather, scholars have argued that there is a reason fundamentalism as a phenomenon – a manifestation common in a variety of religious traditions – is a product of the twentieth century. It itself is as modern as that form of religion it seeks to reject. Mormon fundamentalism is no exception. In its mobilization of nostalgia for the career of Joseph Smith Jr. as a weapon against particular aspects of the modern world; in its economic imagination, which tried to reconcile the idea of the Law of Consecration with contemporary American capitalism; and in its frequent contempt for modernity, Mormon fundamentalism is a quintessentially twentieth-century phenomenon.[71]

Woolley was excommunicated from the LDS church in 1924. By the late 1920s he and several allies began to assemble the Council of Friends. According to Woolley those men selected by John Taylor had in large part died off and needed replacing. As the last surviving member of the Council, he claimed the title of President of the Priesthood and ordained six new members, including Joseph Musser. Woolley died in 1934, but by that point the Council of Friends was well established. The next year, the Council sent a few polygamous families

---

[71] Martin E. Marty and Scott Appleby, eds., *Fundamentalisms Comprehended* (Chicago, IL: University of Chicago Press, 1995); George Marsden, *Fundamentalism and American Culture* (New York: Oxford University Press, 1995).

south from Salt Lake City to a town called Short Creek just over the Utah border into Arizona. Like Brigham Young and his fellows, they hoped that flight to a rural location outside their state's immediate jurisdiction would bring them peace.

By the 1940s, several hundred people lived in Short Creek. Like Brigham Young and Joseph Smith Jr. before him, they tried to establish the Law of Consecration. The Council created the "United Effort Plan," a trust that owned most of the town's properties and businesses, which were operated by members of the community. They also sent their followers to Salt Lake, where they distributed literature and sought more converts. As a result, Short Creek was beginning to attract notice. In response, in 1933 the leadership of the LDS church issued another declaration, called the Final Manifesto. It was read in every LDS congregation, and it denounced polygamy in strong terms. To seek out and cut off those who supported Woolley and the Council of Friends, LDS leaders began to make concerted efforts. In 1935, nearly every member of the LDS ward in Short Creek was excommunicated.[72]

And yet, many polygamists continued to consider themselves part of the LDS church. Joseph Musser, by then living in Short Creek, had a great deal to do with the reason why. Through the 1930s and 1940s, Musser made himself the leading theologian of the fundamentalist movement, largely because of his prolific writings. He published numerous pamphlets and short books that defended the practice of polygamy, explicated the necessity of the United Effort Plan, speculated upon the nature of God, and castigated the LDS church for the various ways Musser believed it had drifted from orthodoxy. He also founded, edited, and was the primary contributor to *Truth Magazine*, a monthly periodical that commented on the news, offered poetry, reprinted sermons from nineteenth-century LDS leaders like Brigham Young, and bound together the many practitioners of polygamy into a single intellectual movement.[73]

Musser presented his emerging theology as the genuine Mormonism practiced in the nineteenth century, but, as with any fundamentalist movement, Musser saw the past through the lenses of the present, which marked the form of fundamentalism he helped to create. First, Musser drew a distinction between the priesthood and the church, though the two were related. The LDS church, he claimed, was indeed God's restored church, and it possessed genuine priesthood authority. However, the LDS church was out of order. Because of that, the Priesthood Council, also known as the Council of Friends among Woolley's followers, had been given priesthood authority higher than the LDS church. The

---

[72] Hardy, *Solemn Covenant*, 341–5.
[73] On Musser's ideas outlined herein, see Rosetti, *Joseph White Musser.*

leadership of the LDS church and the leadership of the priesthood, then, were distinct. The Priesthood Council and its followers were specially charged with keeping polygamy in existence despite the limitations of the church.

These ideas, of course, did not derive from Joseph Smith Jr., but represented a way of reconciling his beliefs about priesthood, polygamy, and restoration with the adaptations that had occurred in the Mormon movement over the previous hundred years. Musser adopted other ideas characteristic of nineteenth-century Mormonism that were beginning to fall out of favor in the LDS church and foregrounded them, making them central to the identity of his movement. Among these was what is popularly known as the "Adam–God doctrine." Brigham Young, believing as he did that human souls were literally the offspring of God the Father and a Heavenly Mother, combined that notion with Joseph Smith's declaration that God was in fact an exalted human, and. arrived at the conclusion that Adam was in fact God the Father, the biological as well as the spiritual father of the human race. Most of Young's contemporaries found this idea confusing, and it faded from the LDS church after Young's death in 1877. But Musser revived and endorsed it, making it a centerpiece of fundamentalist Mormon theology.[74]

Similarly, Musser further cultivated the connections nineteenth-century LDS leaders had made between polygamy and patriarchy, emphasizing that polygamy was essential not simply to leadership in the church on the earth but also in the afterlife. For Musser, not only the practice of polygamy but also the number of wives a man had was linked to spiritual and ecclesiastical authority. He developed a series of laws governing the practice of polygamy in the fundamentalist community, turning it from simply a marriage practice to a governing principle for a social order. Musser claimed these laws were not his; rather, they reflected human nature. He argued polygamy would generate respectful relationships between men and women and the dominance of righteous patriarchs, leading in turn to a righteous and harmonious society. The men who had the most wives would be morally tempered by their marriages, and in turn would be elevated in society, leading a community with wisdom. Polygamy would encourage women to develop loving communities among themselves; they would cooperate in child rearing while men attended to providing. Musser inveighed against birth control and the suffragist movement. Clearly his development of a social philosophy of polygamy might be seen as a response to the changing gender norms of the twentieth century.

---

[74] On the Adam–God doctrine's origins and afterlife, see Gary James Bergera, *Conflict in the Quorum: Orson Pratt, Brigham Young, Joseph Smith* (Salt Lake City, UT: Signature Books, 2002) and Jonathan A Stapley, "Brigham Young's Garden Cosmology," *Journal of Mormon History* 47 (2021), 68–85.

Finally, Musser and other fundamentalists were vehement supporters of Brigham Young's ideas about race. Throughout the mid-twentieth century, the leaders of the LDS church began to grapple with Brigham Young's ban on full participation of Black members, particularly as racial segregation came under increasing fire in the United States in the 1950s and 1960s. Joseph Musser and his contemporaries said little about the issue of race but took for granted that the ban was appropriate. By the 1970s, however, Musser's successors were enunciating vocal support for these racial restrictions, and when the LDS church revoked the ban in 1978, many of them pointed to the change as a further sign of the LDS church's apostasy. As with polygamy, they cultivated an even more detailed justification for the ban than had the LDS church and defended it with language similar to that used by white supremacist groups opposing the desegregation laws of the 1960s.[75]

As fundamentalists coalesced as a coherent social and ideological group in the 1940s, the leaders of the LDS church grew particularly uncomfortable with the existence of the Short Creek settlement. The LDS apostle Mark E. Petersen (1900–1984) is generally credited with coining the term "Mormon fundamentalist" in that decade. For Petersen, as for many Americans in the 1940s, within memory of the media circus of the trial of John Scopes for teaching the theory of evolution in a Tennessee school, the word "fundamentalist" implied a primitive and backward worldview, and that is how he perceived the Short Creek community. Rampant worries in both Utah and Arizona in and out of the LDS church led to the first of two cataclysmic events that drove Mormon fundamentalists further and further away from the LDS church.

On July 26, 1953, with encouragement from the LDS church authorities and the state of Utah, agents of the government of Arizona entered Short Creek and took virtually the entire population of the town – some 400 people – into custody. Public attention was immediate and negative. Photographs of mothers comforting terrified children, elderly men in handcuffs, and women being herded into police vans drew national criticism, as did worry about what would happen to the more than 200 children whose parents faced indictment. In the end, Arizona backed down; three dozen men were given suspended sentences, and though the state hoped to divert the children into foster care, nearly all were returned to their parents. The possibility of future major police actions receded.[76] A decade after the raid the community was renamed "Colorado City, Arizona" with a sister town, Hilldale, just over the Utah line in an attempt to shake off the notoriety of the Short Creek name.

---

[75] Cristina Rosetti, "Not until the Millennium: 1978 and Fundamentalist Whitelash," *American Religion* 3:2 (Spring 2022), 51–68.

[76] Bradley, *Kidnapped from that Land*.

But the impact of the raid was deep and lasting. It intensified the community's suspicion of the outside world and encouraged fundamentalist leaders to nurture separatist tendencies among their followers. In dress and grooming, the community began to embrace traditionalist styles similar to those of the Amish and other Anabaptist traditions. By the mid-twentieth century FLDS leaders were exhorting women to keep their hair long, wear dresses, and avoid makeup or jewelry, while men were told to wear white shirts buttoned to the wrist. By the late twentieth century FLDS leaders discouraged watching television or reading magazines.[77]

These characteristics increasingly came to characterize only a single group of Mormon fundamentalists. On the heels of the raid, the Short Creek community saw a major schism. By the early 1950s Joseph Musser had ascended to the head of the Council of Friends, and shortly before his death in 1954, he suddenly elevated his longtime friend Rulon Allred (1906–1977) as his "counselor" and "second elder," designating Allred as his successor in all but name. The other members of the Council fractured over this breach in protocol, and in 1952, Musser dissolved the Council and ordained six new members, including Allred. Upon Musser's death, the community fragmented. A man named Leroy Johnson (1888–1986) consolidated power in Short Creek, while Allred's followers avoided the town, instead building a community in the Salt Lake Valley.[78]

Leroy Johnson would lead the Short Creek community until his death in 1986 and solidified its slow drift away from the LDS church that had long characterized its history in two ways. Johnson was more comfortable than Musser or Woolley speaking of his group as distinct from the LDS church. Shortly after his death, in 1991 his successors legally incorporated a term he sometimes used: the Fundamentalist Church of Jesus Christ of Latter Day Saints (FLDS). Second, Johnson increasingly consolidated power around himself. Like Musser, he dismissed members of the Council of Friends who opposed his authority. By the end of his life, Johnson embraced what came to be called "the One Man doctrine." Joseph Smith's original revelation teaching polygamy stated that only one person had the authority to solemnize plural marriages at any point in history. From that, Johnson deduced that all authority should rest in a single

---

[77] Ken Driggs, "Twentieth Century Polygamy and Fundamentalist Mormons in Southern Utah," *Dialogue: A Journal of Mormon Thought* 24:4 (1991), 44–58.

[78] The travails of what would become the FLDS church in Short Creek/Colorado City are well documented in Benjamin Bistline, *The Polygamists: A History of Colorado City* (Scottsdale, AZ: Agreka Books, 2004). Craig L. Foster and Marianne Watson, *American Polygamy: A History of Fundamentalist Mormon Faith* (Charleston, SC: The History Press, 2019) discuss both the FLDS church and the AUB, discussed herein.

leader, and he ceased making appointments to the Council of Friends in the 1980s. It was largely defunct by the time of his death.[79]

When Johnson died, the leading member of the Council that remained assumed authority in the FLDS church and took for himself the title of "prophet," a word none of his predecessors had used to refer to themselves. His name was Rulon Jeffs (1909–2002). Upon his death in 2002, his son Warren Jeffs (b. 1955) assumed his authority. Over the first few years of Warren Jeffs's leadership, the FLDS church came under increasing scrutiny from the media and government. Since Johnson's time, the increased insularity of the FLDS community and the rise of the One Man doctrine had produced an evolution in the practice of polygamy. In the practice called "placement" the leader of the FLDS church would arrange marriages among his followers. In 2004, Jeffs excommunicated twenty men from the FLDS church and reassigned their wives and children to other men. Soon, civil lawsuits and media coverage drew attention to the church. In 2005, state officials in Arizona indicted several FLDS men for sexual contact with minors – teenage girls who had been placed as their wives. Over the next few years, Warren Jeffs himself was indicted several times in three different states on charges of rape and child abuse, and in 2011 was convicted and sentenced to life in prison in Texas.

In the aftermath of Jeffs's imprisonment, the FLDS church entered a crisis. State officials in Utah and Texas seized church property. Many of the several thousand members of the FLDS church continued to insist upon allegiance to their imprisoned prophet, rallying around Jeffs's son Helaman as a proxy for his father, but many others abandoned their loyalty to him, forming or joining other fundamentalist movements.[80]

Some transferred their loyalty to the Apostolic United Brethren, the common name for the group that had followed Rulon Allred after Musser's death (though Allred himself called it "the Work"). Under Allred, the AUB rejected the separatism that came to characterize the FLDS church. Most members settled in suburban Salt Lake City, with other, smaller settlements in Mexico and Canada. While Leroy Johnson and the Jeffses drew further and further away from the LDS church, Allred taught that his followers were actually a spiritual part of the church; although they were either excommunicated or never baptized LDS members in the first place, Allred regarded the AUB as a spiritual vanguard keeping polygamy present on the earth. He thus saw no need to do missionary work or temple rituals, telling his followers that the LDS church was handling that aspect of God's affairs.

---

[79] On Johnson's ascendance, Bistline, *The Polygamists*, 64–8.

[80] Stuart A. Wright and Susan J. Palmer, *Storming Zion: Government Raids on Religious Communities* (New York: Oxford University Press, 2016), 153–76.

But that relationship grew tense by the late 1970s. In 1977 Allred was murdered by the LeBaron family, a group of independent polygamists, and his brother Owen assumed leadership of the group. Owen Allred (1914–2005) was infuriated by the LDS church's 1978 revocation of the ban on full participation of people of African descent in the church and declared that because Black people would now be participating in them, LDS temple rituals were profaned. The AUB thus began constructing its own temples and performing its own rites in the 1980s.

The AUB movement is similar in size to the FLDS church, but unlike the FLDS, the AUB seek integration with the communities around them. Owen Allred, having seen the legal challenges that bedeviled the RLDS church, sought transparency with law enforcement and Utah politicians, willingly sharing information with the state government and asking only to be left alone. Rulon Allred had rejected the practice of placement marriages, instead promoting courtship, and that only of people of legal age. Similarly, though the AUB operates several charter schools, AUB children sometimes attend public schools and their dress is only slightly more conservative than those of their classmates.[81]

The murder of Rulon Allred indicates the variety of Mormon fundamentalisms. Aside from the FLDS and the AUB, a number of smaller fundamentalist movements exist, and many do not trace their roots to Lorin Woolley's Council of Friends. The Latter Day Church of Christ was organized in northern Utah by the family of Charles Kingston (1884–1975), who, after a meeting with Lorin Woolley, rejected the LDS church's abandonment of polygamy. He and his sons built their own cooperative polygamous society with several hundred followers and have attracted prosecution for reasons not unlike those that dog the FLDS church.

But many other fundamentalist movements claim authority from independent prophetic and visionary experience rather than a mere application of Lorin Woolley's claims. The family of Alma Dyer LeBaron Sr. (1886–1951) was affiliated with Council of Friends until the mid-1950s, when several of LeBaron's sons declared they had received revelatory experiences entrusting them with divine authority. They organized the Church of the Firstborn in 1955, but quickly fell into violence and infighting. Their church still exists, with a strong enclave in northern Mexico. Similarly, in 1994 Jim Harmston (1940–2013) of Manti, Utah, formed the True and Living Church of Jesus Christ of Saints of the Last Days after God revealed to him that all churches on earth,

---

[81] The AUB's attention to public relations is ably discussed in Janet Bennion, *Polygamy in Primetime: Media, Gender and Politics in Mormon Fundamentalism* (Lebanon, NH: University Press of New England, 2012), 36–9.

including the LDS church Harmston belonged to, were corrupt. After that revelation Harmston was ordained to the true priesthood by the resurrected patriarchs Moses, Abraham, and Noah. Vigorous proselyting gained Harmston several hundred followers, and he introduced polygamy among them and taught that the Second Coming of Jesus Christ was imminent before his death in 2013. At least a dozen other such groups exist as well.[82]

These smaller fundamentalist movements share many common characteristics with the larger fundamentalist Mormon churches. All teach the Adam–God doctrine, some form of the Law of Consecration, and polygamy. Most, like Owen Allred, believe that the LDS church was wrong to allow the full participation of people of African descent. And most also, like other fundamentalist believers, urge some degree of resistance to the modern world, presenting themselves as conservators of an imagined and ideal Mormon past.

Set in parallel, then, these three versions of Mormonism illustrate what a number of religious studies scholars have observed: new religious movements pursue a variety of positions in relationship with the culture in which they find themselves. Resistance and accommodation each offer benefits. The RLDS church was able to expand and claim control of the Kirtland temple in part because it seemed amenable to the Protestants who ran the American government. On the other hand, the fundamentalist movement has been able to cultivate strong loyalties, and has proven capable of generating charismatic leader after charismatic leader, despite official government repression.

4 The Emergence of Mormon Studies

The earliest works of history of the Mormon movement were characteristic of nineteenth-century "church" or "denominational history" – that is, produced for the use of religious communities and commonly produced among American Protestant denominations. Much of it predated the emergence of professionalized standards of scholarship.[83] As such, they tended to defend the restorationist claims of these various denominations, and to define their histories in relation to the patterns of culture that surrounded them. As these studies began to intersect with the work of professional scholars of religion, however, researchers with less personal investment in the life of these communities began to see

---

[82] Steven Shields, *Divergent Paths of the Restoration: An Encyclopedia of the Smith–Rigdon Movement* (Salt Lake City, UT: Signature Books, 2022). This is the fifth edition of Shields's exhaustive study of the many branches of Mormonism.

[83] On this definition of "church history" see Martin Marty, *The Writing of American Religious History* (New York: KG Sauer, 1992); Jerald Brauer, "Changing Perspectives on Religion in America," in Jerald Brauer, ed., *Reinterpretation in American Church History* (Chicago, IL: University of Chicago, 1968), 1–19.

Mormonism as a useful mode for studying the phenomenon of new religious movements in the United States.

There are a number of parallels among the insider histories of the LDS and Community of Christ communities. Both the LDS and the RLDS churches produced official histories early in their existence. Beginning in 1832, Joseph Smith worked with various followers to produce a history of his movement, and in Nauvoo dutiful secretaries kept an official journal for him. In 1839, after various false starts, the first project finally took hold. Some portions were published in the church's newspapers in Nauvoo, and Brigham Young's followers carried the completed pages cross the plains with them to Salt Lake City. There Young appointed a series of official historians to combine the journal and these various earlier efforts into an outright history of the life of Joseph Smith and his movement until his death. In 1856, it was completed; it is today known as *The Manuscript History of the Church*, published in six volumes for a total of approximately 2500 pages in the original.

In 1901 the LDS historian and General Authority Brigham Henry Roberts (1857–1933) took on the task of re-editing and expanding the *Manuscript History*. He made his way through the six published volumes, adding an extensive introduction to each and commentary in footnotes. He also performed extensive silent revision and added a final volume which covered Brigham Young's ascension to the leadership of the LDS church and his organization of the church's migration to Salt Lake City between 1844 and 1848. Roberts completed the task by 1912. At almost the same time, he began his own project, a history covering Joseph Smith's life and the history of the LDS church through the early twentieth century, published in multiple parts in the *American Historical Magazine*. He made some revisions and the LDS church published the history for the anniversary of Joseph Smith's organization of the church in 1930. This is sometimes called the *Comprehensive History of the Church of Jesus Christ of Latter-day Saints*.

At roughly the same time that Roberts was engaged in his labors, Joseph Smith III and the RLDS apostle Heman Smith (1850–1919) began work on *The History of the Reorganized Church of Jesus Christ of Latter-day Saints*. Published in four volumes between 1897 and 1903, it covered the period until the end of the nineteenth century. In 1934, Heman Smith's daughter Inez Smith Davis (1889–1954) condensed that history into her own *The Story of the Church*, taking the narrative up through the presidency of Frederick Madison Smith. In 1943 and 1948, she expanded the book to take it up to the present day.

Comparing the histories produced by the writers of the *Manuscript History* and Roberts with the two Smiths and Davis reveals that all of these narratives are what might be called denominational histories. They are written first with what the authors perceived to be the interest and identity of their denominations in mind. Thus, Roberts's work draws upon the LDS perception of persecution, which had become central to his denomination's identity during the prosecutions of polygamy, setting his church against a presumably corrupt American culture. He elevates Joseph Smith's own suffering, emphasizes that other Americans consistently rejected and persecuted Mormons, and links that persecution to practices like polygamy, the Law of Consecration, and building temples. For Roberts, then, persecution is a sign of Joseph Smith's independence, inspiration, and access to divine truth.

Just so, the RLDS authors seek to downplay the beliefs and practices of Joseph Smith Jr. that inspired opposition among non-Mormons. Smith III, Herman Smith, and Davis all pin the blame for polygamy on John C. Bennett (1804–1867), an erstwhile ally of Joseph Smith Jr. whom the prophet excommunicated and ejected from Nauvoo for sleeping with numerous married Mormon women. In 1842, Bennett published a lurid exposé accusing Smith of the same. While for Roberts a defiant, radical, polygamous Joseph Smith is of denominational use, for the RLDS authors a Joseph Smith acceptable to respectable Protestant Americans is of significant importance, and Bennett is a useful scapegoat for preserving Smith's reputation. Likewise, they also downplay those ideas and practices Smith presented in Nauvoo that the RLDS church later rejected, like temple worship and the embodiment of God.

In the mid-twentieth century this denominational history began to be displaced. In 1969, the scholar Moses Rischin identified what he called the "New Mormon History."[84] According to Rischin, history writing about the Mormon churches had moved beyond denominational histories. Instead, scholars with academic training had taken the topic on and were producing work meeting the standards of the profession.

As evidence, Rischin cited the emergence of independent scholarly organizations. In particular, he referred to the Mormon History Association, organized in 1965, and *Dialogue: A Journal of Mormon Thought*. MHA began publishing an academic journal, the *Journal of Mormon History* in 1974. Both venues published peer-reviewed scholarship and served as the chief hubs for academic work on the Mormon tradition that often rejected or bracketed the question of Joseph Smith's divine inspiration.

The New Mormon History is often dated to the publication of Fawn Brodie's biography *No Man Knows My History: The Life of Joseph Smith* (1945). Brodie followed in the wake of a number of early twentieth-century studies of Joseph

---

[84] Moses Rischin, "The New Mormon History," *American West* 6:2 (1969), 49. The essay is one page long.

Smith, such as I. Woodbridge Riley's *The Founder of Mormonism: A Psychological Study of Joseph Smith* (1902) and William Linn's *The Story of the Mormons*, published the same year. Riley and Linn took for granted that Mormonism was the product of dysfunction, a deviation from the American norm. For Riley, Joseph Smith was an epileptic and his religion the product of Smith's seizure visions. For Linn, cynical and manipulative Mormon leaders preyed upon the blind faith of ignorant followers.

Brodie's interpretation was more complex than these. Her research was thorough and she took seriously the notion that Joseph Smith was not in some way sui generis but the product of antebellum American religious culture. She rejected the notion that Joseph Smith was a genuine prophet, instead arguing that he was a gifted fabulist, desperate to rise above his family's economic struggles, who came to believe his own fictions. In this way, Brodie showed how embedded Smith was in the folk Christianity and visionary culture of antebellum American culture; his movement gained followers because it spoke to the needs and questions of the religious world he lived in. The book took Joseph Smith's religious work seriously, if not literally, and in so doing paved the way for serious academic study of Mormonism.

Brodie was the niece of David O. McKay, who served as president of the LDS church from 1951 to 1970; despite his fondness for her, she was excommunicated in 1946. Much of the New Mormon History was produced by people like Brodie – Mormons with academic training (Brodie held an M.A. from the University of Chicago) who strove to produce professional work but whose perceptions were also marked by their relationship with the tradition. Two good examples are Juanita Brooks and Robert Flanders. Like Brodie, Brooks was a member of the LDS church. She held a master's degree from Columbia and worked at Dixie College in southern Utah before pursuing her research and writing. Robert Flanders held a PhD from the University of Wisconsin and taught history at Graceland College, owned by the RLDS church.

Both scholars produced work that was professionally responsible but challenged some pieties in their respective traditions. Brooks's *The Mountain Meadows Massacre* (1950) and Flanders's *Nauvoo: Kingdom on the Mississippi* (1965) each reflected a tradition's unsettled feelings about the past, grappling with points of tension and controversy. When Brooks began her book, common wisdom in the LDS church still blamed the massacre on Native Americans and a few rogue white members of the Church. She carefully pieced together the story of the leaders of the southern Utah LDS community who planned the massacre, arguing that they acted out of fear of outsiders stoked by Brigham Young and other LDS leaders. Flanders delicately picked his way through the Nauvoo period, defying RLDS conventional wisdom by accepting that polygamy's origins lay with Joseph Smith and chronicling Smith's interest in temple rituals, baptism for the dead, and other practices the RLDS had rejected. Brooks saw the production of her book as something of an expiation for her southern Utah community; Flanders told the story of Nauvoo as a tragedy – a moment where a prophet's reach exceeded his grasp. It was a cautionary tale.

By the 1970s, the New Mormon History movement had to some degree become established in both the LDS and RLDS churches. In 1966, Richard Howard, who held a graduate degree in history from the University of California–Berkeley, was appointed church historian to the RLDS church. In 1972, Leonard Arrington, who held a PhD from the University of North Carolina, was appointed church historian and director of the History Division of the church Historical Department in the LDS church. Both men sought to professionalize the writing of history in their tradition, and to introduce the products of professional historical research into the devotional and spiritual life of each denomination, with sometimes painful results. Howard's book *Restoration Scriptures: A Study of Their Textual Development* (1969) evaluated Joseph Smith's production of scripture, arguing that textual study of the various editions of the Book of Mormon and published revelations in Joseph Smith's lifetime revealed that Smith understood the text to have a dynamic quality consistent with his notion of revelation. Arrington's *Great Basin Kingdom: An Economic History of the Latter-day Saints, 1830–1900* (1950) linked the economic organization of the LDS settlement of early Utah to the communal ideas implicit in LDS theology. He found that LDS irrigation practices were central not simply to the economic organization of Utah, but to its religious and cultural irrigation as well. Both books received acclaim by other professional historians.

Howard and Arrington inspired the work of a number of other historians in each denomination. Indeed, the New Mormon History flourished in the 1980s and early 1990s. Thomas Alexander, D. Michael Quinn, Valeen Tippetts Avery, Linda King Newell, William Russell, Paul Edwards, and many other scholars in both movements received professional training and produced New Mormon History of great value. Avery and Newell's biography *Mormon Enigma: Emma Hale Smith* (1984) was the first major work of feminist scholarship on the Mormon tradition, drawing on feminist techniques and methodologies of primary source reading to recover and reconstruct the life of Joseph Smith Jr.'s wife Emma, who left little in the way of firsthand primary sources. In so doing, Avery and Newell set a pattern for exploring women's history in the LDS church: it explored polygamy, the impact of a patriarchal priesthood leadership, and how women sought to exercise agency in such conditions.

Other works of New Mormon history offered essential institutional history. In the early 1990s Quinn produced a pair of volumes called *The Mormon Hierarchy* that explored the origins and foundation of LDS priestly leadership. (He added a third in 2017.) Gregory Prince, B. Carmon Hardy, Alexander, and Russell produced essential studies of institutional development. Prince produced volumes on the administration of LDS president David O. McKay and Arrington's tenure as Church Historian. Alexander's *Mormonism in Transition: A History of the Latter-day Saints, 1890–1930* traced the transformation of the LDS church from a sect on the fringe of American culture to the established denomination it had become by the mid-twentieth century. B. Carmon Hardy told a similar story in his *Solemn Covenant: The Mormon Polygamous Passage*, which documented the LDS church's slow abandonment of polygamy. William Russell's series of articles on the relationship between the RLDS and the LDS church over the twentieth century highlighted how many scholars and leaders understood the two movements, while Paul Edwards's work on the life and administration of Frederick Madison Smith showed how the RLDS church similarly transformed itself into a modern institution.

Howard and Arrington's work also produced some tension within their respective denominations. Arrington orchestrated an official history of the LDS church, *The Story of the Latter-day Saints*, published in 1976 by the church-owned press, Deseret Book, along with a companion volume *The Mormon Experience: A History of the Latter-day Saints*, published in 1979 by Knopf and intended for audiences unfamiliar with the LDS tradition. Arrington himself and another church historian, Davis Bitton, wrote the second volume, while James Allen and Glen Leonard wrote the first. The first book earned the praise of some LDS officials, but attracted vocal criticism from others, who objected to the authors' failure to attribute the LDS church's success solely to the will of God in particular – but more broadly – Arrington's attempt to institute conventional professional historical standards in denominationally-sponsored history writing. Similarly, by the early 1980s Howard was convinced that, despite long-standing RLDS understanding, Joseph Smith had, in fact, begun the practice of polygamy in the Mormon tradition. Many RLDS leaders were uncomfortable with Howard's published defense of that position.

By the mid-1980s, Arrington had been moved to a position at Brigham Young University, and over the next few years, several LDS officials instigated an attempt to reassert traditional faithful history-telling in that denomination. Some scholars were forced from positions at Brigham Young University. Two of these and several others were excommunicated in 1993, and in the LDS church, the New Mormon History entered a period of hibernation. On the other hand, when Howard retired in 1994, he was replaced by Mark Scherer, who earned a PhD from the University of Missouri–Kansas City. Both Scherer and Howard produced multivolume histories of the RLDS church: Howard in a constellation of essays and Scherer in narrative form. Howard tentatively pushed the boundaries of denominational history, raising the issue of polygamy and Joseph Smith's self-destructive behavior; Scherer amplified these issues in his own writing, and retained the institutional support of the RLDS (and, later, Community of Christ) leadership.

In 2005, Knopf published Richard Bushman's magisterial *Joseph Smith: Rough Stone Rolling*. In the *Journal of American History*, Jan Shipps called the biography "the crowing achievement of the New Mormon History."[85] By this she meant the book was meticulously researched, carefully written, deeply embedded in the historiography – just as one might have expected from Bushman, Gouverneur Morris Professor of History at Columbia University, the author of a number of celebrated works on early American history, and a member of the LDS church. For Bushman, Smith was best understood as a visionary who grappled with many of the challenges of the early American republic, from the destabilizing effects of the emerging market economy to the culture of honor that governed interactions among Americans aspiring to respectability. Smith's new religious movement could be understood as a mode of response to these things. At the same time, Bushman frankly admitted his belief that Smith was inspired, and he was clear that his book was a response to Brodie, building on her work while at the same time contesting her thesis that Smith was to some extent a conscious fraud. *Rough Stone Rolling* is far more deeply researched than *No Man Knows My History*, but it is also, inevitably, indebted to the earlier book.

Shipps's judgment is revealing, because in many ways, her own work pointed toward what might lie beyond the New Mormon History. *Mormonism: The Story of a New Religious Tradition* (1985) presaged much of where Mormon studies would go in the next four decades. Indeed, it perhaps signaled the emergence of something called "Mormon studies"; broader than, but encompassing, the New Mormon History.

New Mormon History continues to be produced, of course. In fact, by the first years of the twenty-first century, the LDS Church Historical Department had for the most part reversed its suspicion of academic history and began devoting substantial resources to the production of professional, if devotional, history. Most notable was the Joseph Smith Papers Project, a two-decade-long effort to compile, edit, and provide source notes and commentary for every document

---

[85] Jan Shipps, "Richard Lyman Bushman, the Story of Joseph Smith and Mormonism, and the New Mormon History," *Journal of American History* 94:2 (2007), 498–516.

Joseph Smith produced or supervised across his lifetime. Eventually producing twenty-seven volumes, and publishing many more documents online, the project has received wide praise from across the academic community for its accuracy and transparency.

At the same time, many scholars in the field had begun moving in new directions. Several aspects differentiated Shipps's work from that which came before, and signaled where historiography would move in the twenty-first century. Shipps was among the first modern scholars of religion who took an interest in Mormonism while belonging to no Mormon tradition. (Scholars like Wallace Stegner and Mark Leone wrote earlier than Shipps, but her work has proven more influential on the academic study of Mormonism.) Unlike many New Mormon Historians, then, her interest in Mormonism derived from broader questions that haunted the discipline of religious studies about the meaning of religion, how religious communities legitimize themselves to their followers and to outside authorities, and how they relate to American culture writ large. To do this, Shipps drew on a wide range of theory of religion. The work of Mircea Eliade is foundational for her in *Mormonism*; she also draws upon the classic church–sect typology developed by early twentieth-century scholars of religion like Max Weber. These are two central figures in the modern study of religion. Eliade's work explores what he takes to be the primal patterns of the human religious impulse, finding a quest for the pure perfection of the moment of the creation of the world at the heart of much religious ritual. Weber was a key contributor to much theory about the development of religion, arguing for a juxtaposition between sects – small separatist religious groups – and churches – larger organizations comfortable in the world around them. In *Mormonism*, Shipps argues that early Mormons sought to separate themselves from the rest of American culture through a reenactment of the Hebrew Bible, only eventually to abandon the effort through reintegration with the rest of American society. This story, she says, might demonstrate a great deal about how new religious movements fail or succeed.

Over the twenty or so years after the publication of *Mormonism: The Story of a New Religious Tradition*, a series of works evaluating the Mormon tradition as Shipps had – as illustrating or exemplifying broader issues with the place of religion in American public life – emerged. Signaling the breadth of interest this work attracted, much of it was published, as was Shipps's book, by university presses. The University of Illinois Press, which published Shipps, maintained a strong list in Mormon studies throughout the 1990s, and revived it late in the 2010s when the University of North Carolina Press and Oxford University Press began publishing in the field as well.

Chief among the works published by these presses were Kathleen Flake's *The Politics of American Religious Identity: The Seating of Senator Reed Smoot, Mormon Apostle* (2004), Sarah Barringer Gordon's *The Mormon Question: Polygamy and Constitutional Conflict in Nineteenth Century America* (2001), Armand Mauss's *The Angel and the Beehive: The Mormon Struggle with Assimilation* (1994), and Philip Barlow's *Mormons and the Bible: The Place of the Latter-day Saints in American Religion* (1991). Each of these works departed from the New Mormon History's tight focus on the Mormon tradition itself, instead treating Mormonism as an example to illustrate other conundrums in the history of religion in America. Significantly, none of these authors were historians. Barlow and Flake were trained in religious studies; Mauss was a sociologist; and Gordon a legal scholar. Each piece of work had a strong methodological orientation, and thus was targeted at distinct theoretical questions.

For Flake and Gordon, the LDS church was a useful example to explore how American law and politics came to discipline religion in the late nineteenth- and early twentieth-century United States. Distaste for polygamy and worry about the political and economic influence of the LDS hierarchy led the US federal court system and Congress to investigate and eventually circumscribe these aspects of the LDS church, forcing it eventually to adapt and come to resemble a Protestant denomination. In so doing, Flake and Gordon draw larger observations about how religion in the United States is consciously defined and governed by American institutions – the state chief among them. Mauss and Barlow make similar observations. Barlow argues that the LDS relationship with the Bible illustrates a simultaneous desire to be considered a genuine Christian denomination, but also to assert its theological distinctiveness. Mauss contends that the course of twentieth-century LDS history demonstrates a similar vacillation between sectarian and churchly tendencies, the desire for respectability and esteem, and the desire for independence and particularity. While Flake and Gordon observe the American state disciplining religious movements, Barlow and Mauss show how those movements themselves exert agency in their expressions.

These works inaugurated a modern renaissance in Mormon studies. Its interest in questions beyond those emerging from within the Mormon tradition itself has deeply impacted the work of contemporary historians of the Mormon tradition. Some of these have revisited points of interest to earlier historians, placing them in new contexts and drawing differing interpretations. Benjamin Park's *Kingdom of Nauvoo: The Rise and Fall of a Religious Empire on the American Frontier* (2020) takes a new look at the Mormon time in Nauvoo, linking Joseph Smith's ambitions there to a broader debate over the nature of democracy in antebellum America. Similarly, Thomas Simpson's *American Universities and the Birth of Modern Mormonism* (2016) intertwines the LDS church's abandonment of polygamy and assimilation into the United States with the history of higher education in America, showing how the emerging university system served as a grounds for church authorities to reconceptualize what Mormonism was. Jared Farmer's *On Zion's Mount: Mormons, Indians and the American Landscape* (2008) offered a cultural history of Mount Timpanogos, a landmark Utah mountain whose invented history illustrates the complex history of LDS–Native interactions.

But beyond these works, gradually the field has pushed beyond its traditional focus on history to other methodologies and broader questions.

For instance, beginning with the scholar of literature Terryl Givens's *By the Hand of Mormon: The American Scripture that Launched a New World Religion* (2003), a number of scholars of religion and literature have paid increasing attention to the Book of Mormon, and by extension, Mormonism as a literary tradition. Givens's book both treated the text of the Book of Mormon and, famously, argued for its importance as an object as well – a signifier of Joseph Smith's religious authority that continues to be wielded. Givens has followed up *By the Hand of Mormon* with a number of other studies of Mormonism in general and the LDS tradition in particular, offering scholarly analyses of Mormon culture (*People of Paradox: A History of Mormon Culture*, 2010) and nineteenth-century LDS theology (the diptych *Foundations of Mormon Thought*, including the two volumes *Wrestling the Angel*, 2015, and *Feeding the Flock*, 2017*)*. Givens centers his work on a dynamic, romantic interpretation of Mormon culture, rooting Joseph Smith in the nineteenth-century Romantic tradition.

Subsequent works have begun to take the Book of Mormon seriously as a text, drawing on Grant Hardy's *Understanding the Book of Mormon* (2003), a painstakingly close read of the book that argues for its complex literary qualities. The scholars of literature Jared Hickman and Elizabeth Fenton have applied contemporary literary theory to the text in their *Americanist Approaches to the Book of Mormon* (2019), while Joseph Spencer and Michael Austin have made the case for its complex intertextual relationship with the Bible in their respective *A Word in Season: Isaiah's Reception in the Book of Mormon* (2023) and *A Testimony of Two Nations: How the Book of Mormon Reads and Rereads the Bible* (2024).

A number of works have followed Flake and Gordon's exploration of Mormonism and the meaning of religion in the United States. For instance, Spencer Fluhman's *A Peculiar People: Mormonism and the Making of Religion in Nineteenth Century America* (2012) and Peter Coviello's *Make Yourselves*

Gods: Mormons and the Unfinished Work of American Secularism (2019) each take as their premise that religion in the United States is constructed by reigning cultural and institutional powers. The case of Mormonism illustrates how religious movements might challenge and then be disciplined by these authorities. For both Fluhman and Coviello, then, opposition to Mormonism among American Protestants and in American institutions has less to do with Mormonism itself than with the reigning principles of "good" and "bad" religion in American life. David Walker's *Railroading Religion: Mormons, Tourists, and the Corporate Spirit of the West* (2019) showed how the LDS church drew on the arrival of the railroad in Utah and the burgeoning tourist industry to transform itself into an acceptable American religion.

Similarly, a number of works on fundamentalist Mormonism have used it as an example to explore broad questions of the limits state power can place on new religious movements. Martha Sonntag Bradley's 1993 *Kidnapped from that Land: The Government Raids on the Short Creek Polygamists* offered a tight analysis of early Mormon fundamentalism and its 1940s and 1950s confrontations with state governments in Utah and Arizona. More recently, Stuart A. Wright and Susan Palmer's work focuses on the FLDS church and Warren Jeffs's confrontation with federal authorities in the mid-2000s. *Storming Zion: Government Raids on Religious Communities* (2016) compares the FLDS movement to other new religious movements in the United States and elsewhere whose practices have violated various national norms to the point of attracting government intervention.

This central insight understands the fracturing of Mormonism into various traditions as the product of confrontation with and adaptation to broader American ideas about religion. It dates to the work of Shipps and Alexander in the 1980s, but it has shaped much work since, from Flake to Coviello. It also marks much more recent work on Mormonism dealing with other topics, like race and gender.

The most convincing recent works dealing with the Mormon movement and race in the United States are Paul Reeve's *Religion of a Different Color: Race and the Mormon Struggle for Whiteness* (2014), Max Perry Mueller's *Race and the Making of the Mormon People* (2017), and Quincy Newell's *Your Sister in the Gospel: The Life of Jane Manning James, A Nineteenth Century Black Mormon* (2019). Similar works, such as Hokolani Aikau's *A Chosen People, A Promised Land: Mormonism and Race in Hawai'i* (2012), Amanda Hendrix-Komoto's *Imperial Zions: Religion, Race, and Family in the American West and Pacific* (2022), and Elisa Eastwood Pulido's *The Spiritual Evolution of Margarito Bautista: Mexican Mormon Evangelizer, Polygamist Dissident, and Utopian Founder, 1878–1961* (2019), deal with Mormonism and indigeneity beyond the United States. Each of these works builds upon earlier work on Mormonism and race, like that of Newell Bringhurst and Lester Bush as well as that of Mark Scherer. These scholars' work fits squarely in the realm of New Mormon History, carefully documenting the racism of early Mormon leaders and the gradual institutionalization of racist policies in the LDS church and the relative inclusivity of the RLDS church.

But this more recent work, drawing on critical race theory, emphasizes the contingent and cultural nature of "race" as a constructed way to sort and order human beings, linked to concepts of civilization, hierarchy, and power. Rather than simply chronicling the LDS or RLDS churches' racial policies, the work of these scholars emphasizes how the Mormon movement participated in the construction of race or was racialized itself. Reeve, Newell, and Mueller argue that early Mormon ideas about race shifted over time; that early Mormons constructed racial ideas out of the broader stuff of American culture, but combined those ideas with the material of their own theology. For early Mormons, Native Americans were "Lamanites," a people described in the Book of Mormon. For early LDS people, African Americans were descended from Cain and thus were unable to hold priesthood office or engage in temple rites. These modes of racialization extended or sometimes contradicted broader American perceptions of race. Similarly, for Reeve and Perry, as the LDS (and also the RLDS) churches began to seek greater incorporation into American life, they had to adopt increasingly conventional American racial categories.

Similarly, more and more scholars who engage with race and the Mormon tradition reach beyond the United States. Scholars like Aikau and Hendrix-Komoto link the processes of racialization to settler colonialism, showing how Mormons both engaged with and extended the national imperial ambitions of the United States in a similar pattern. In this sense, Mormonism exemplifies in many ways the processes of imperialism and colonialism, while also on occasion bending American imperialism to the ambitions of its own religious imperialism.

Similar processes are at work in the Mormon historiography of gender. The New Mormon Studies produced a number of foundational works on Mormon women's history. Claudia Bushman, Lavina Fielding Anderson, Carol Cornwall Madsen, Maureen Ursenbach Beecher, and Rita Lester produced a great deal of Mormon women's history in the RLDS and LDS churches in the 1970s, 1980s, and 1990s. Two edited collections – *Mormon Sisters: Women in Utah* (1997) and *Sisters in Spirit: Mormon Women in Historical and Cultural Perspective* (1987) – did the initial work of excavating the past of LDS women, as did Martha Bradley's *Pedestals and Podiums: Utah Women, Religious Authority, and Equal Rights* (2005), which explored the impact of second-wave feminism on LDS women.

More recent work on Mormonism and gender has expanded theoretical perspectives past simply "women's history" to consider gender as a constructed cultural category. William Russell's *Homosexual Saints: The Community of Christ Experience* (2008) explores how the RLDS church and eventually the Community of Christ imagined the category of "homosexuality"; similarly, Taylor Petrey's *Tabernacles of Clay: Gender and Sexuality in Modern Mormonism* (2020) does the same for the LDS church, exploring how categories of sexuality and gender changed in the eighty years between the end of World War II and the present. Colleen McDannell's *Sister Saints: Mormon Women since the End of Polygamy* (2018) explores how LDS church leaders generated and enforced traditional gender roles, but also how LDS women understood, embraced, or sometimes subverted those categories. All of these works implicitly embrace the Shipps–Alexander hypothesis, positing that Mormons initially rejected but eventually came to embrace the normative standards of American society. But K. Mohrman's *Exceptionally Queer: Mormon Peculiarity and US Nationalism* (2022) subverts that presumption, arguing that from Joseph Smith's time Mormonism has always incorporated and toyed with elements of American culture writ large, developing an ongoing relationship with American culture that is sometimes more peculiar than other times.

Work like Mohrman's, Aikau's, and Hendrix-Komoto's also points to an emerging field in Mormon studies: that of globalization. Much of this work, like that of these authors, is bound up with notions of imperialism and settler colonialism – the modes by which Mormon missions of all sorts serve as imperial ventures and extend American as well as Mormon coloniality. Joanna Brooks and Gina Colvin's edited collection, *Decolonizing Mormonism* (2018), speaks to these notions from both scholarly and participant perspectives, while the work of anthropologist Thomas Murphy focuses on Mormonism's relationship with indigenous peoples in the American West and in Mexico.

Other contemporary scholars have explored how globalization has changed the nature of the various churches of the Mormon tradition. Caroline Kline's *Mormon Women at the Crossroads: Global Narratives and the Power of Connectedness* (2022) emphasizes how LDS women around the world find different resources and opportunities in the church, premised on the establishment of a female community. Melissa Inouye has produced a series of articles exploring how LDS globalization illustrates the hypotheses of theorist of globalization Roland Robertson, who suggested that "globalization" is better understood as "glocalization."[86] While large-scale institutions, like corporation and religious organizations, might be present around the globe, in each place they find themselves they adapt to local cultures in meaningful ways. David Howlett has also produced a series of articles exploring the globalization of the RLDS church through the mid-twentieth century.[87] For Howlett, following scholars of liberal Protestantism like David Hollinger, the RLDS church across the twentieth century came to value religious pluralism and hence bent its efforts at expansion toward productive engagement with local peoples around the world, and sought to wed their work to international organizations they perceived as promoting charity and human flourishing.

5 Conclusion

In 1992, the religious studies scholar Harold Bloom called Mormonism the "authentic version of the American Religion."[88] What struck Bloom, and many scholars since, about the faith tradition was its democratic, individualist, seemingly romantic conception of humanity. Bloom was dazzled by Joseph Smith's audacity at producing new scripture, reading him as the quintessential American in his capacity for self-creation, defiance of traditional pieties, orthodoxies, and institutions. This is an interpretation that has garnered sympathy from influential, if older, works of scholarship that read nineteenth-century Mormonism as a radical act of democracy in a democratic, Jacksonian nation.[89]

It has also become clear that more recent scholars reject Bloom's interpretation of Mormonism, and instead understand the tradition in more complicated ways. For Bloom, the contemporary LDS church was not genuinely Mormon because it had embraced American capitalism, institutional organization, hierarchies of race and gender, and power.[90] But more recent scholarship on the Mormon tradition has come to see those very aspects that Bloom disdained as part and parcel of the Mormon project in its totality, just as they also mark the American project.

Indeed, understanding the Mormon movement as a new religious movement means that rather than, like Bloom, seeking some essential core to Mormonism,

---

[86] Melissa Inouye, "The Oak and the Banyan: The Glocalization of Mormon Studies," *Mormon Studies Review* 1:1 (2014), 70–9.

[87] David Howlett, "Why Denominations Can Climb Hills: RLDS Conversions in Highland Tribal India and Midwestern America, 1964–2001," *Church History: Studies in Christianity and Culture* 89:3 (2020), 633–58.

[88] Harold Bloom, *The American Religion: The Emergence of the Postchristian Nation* (New York: Simon and Schuster, 1992), 97.

[89] See, for instance, Nathan O. Hatch, *The Democratization of American Christianity* (New Haven, CT: Yale University Press, 1989) and Sydney Ahlstrom, *A Religious History of the American People*, 2nd ed. (New Haven, CT: Yale University Press, 2004), 502–7.

[90] Bloom is clear on this point in *American Religion*, 82–3.

scholars today will seek to understand it as a way to better understand its context, both American and global. The varying branches of Mormonism that have emerged, withered, and thrived point both to the functions varying communities have hoped religion might perform and to the boundaries they have placed upon what religion might be. The differing responses differing branches of Mormonism have offered to American culture writ large illustrate both of these things. If Mormonism is the quintessential American religion, it may be less because of any inherent quality it might exhibit, and more because it illustrates the questions and problems of studying religion in the United States as well as any other.

Bibliography

Abzug, R. 1994. *Cosmos Crumbling: American Reform and the Religious Imagination*. New York: Oxford University Press.

Ahlstrom, S. 2004. *A Religious History of the American People*. New Haven, CT: Yale University Press.

Aikau, H. 2012. *A Chosen People, a Promised Land: Mormonism and Race in Hawai'i*. Minneapolis, MN: University of Minnesota Press.

Alexander, T. 1986. *Mormonism in Transition: A History of the Latter-day Saints, 1890–1930*. Urbana, IL: University of Illinois Press.

Allen, C. L and R. T. Hughes. 1988. *Illusions of Innocent: Protestant Primitivism in America, 1630–1875*. Chicago, IL: University of Chicago Press.

Allen, J. and G. Leonard. 1976. *The Story of the Latter-day Saints*. Salt Lake City, UT: Published in collaboration with the Historical Department of the Church of Jesus Christ of Latter-day Saints by Deseret Book.

Arrington, L. 1958. *Great Basin Kingdom: An Economic History of the Latter-day Saints, 1830–1900*. Cambridge, MA: Harvard University Press.

Arrington, L. and D. Bitton. 1979. *The Mormon Experience: A History of the Latter-day Saints*. New York: Alfred A. Knopf.

Arrington, L., D. May and F. Fox. 1992. *Building the Kingdom of God: Community and Cooperation among the Mormons*. Urbana, IL: University of Illinois Press.

Austin, M. 2024. *Testimony of Two Nations: How the Book of Mormon Reads, and Rereads, the Bible*. Urbana, IL: University of Illinois Press.

Avery, V. and L. Newell. 1984. *Mormon Enigma: Emma Hale Smith*. Urbana, IL: University of Illinois Press.

Barlow, P. 1991. *Mormons and the Bible: The Place of the Latter-day Saints in American Religion*. New York: Oxford University Press.

Beecher, M. and L. Anderson. 1987. *Sisters in Spirit: Mormon Women in Historical and Cultural Perspective*. Urbana, IL: University of Illinois Press.

Bistline, B. 2004. *The Polygamists: A History of Colorado City*. Scottsdale, AZ: Agreka Books.

Bloom, H. 1992. *The American Religion: The Emergence of the Postchristian Nation*. New York: Simon and Schuster.

Bowman, M. 2012. *The Mormon People: The Making of an American Faith*. New York: Random House.

Bradley, M. S. 1993. *Kidnapped from that Land: The Government Raids on the Short Creek Polygamists*. Salt Lake City, UT: University of Utah Press.

Bradley, M. S. 2005. *Pedestals and Podium: Utah Women, Religious Authority, and Equal Rights*. Salt Lake City, UT: Signature Books.

Brodie, F. 1945. *No Man Knows My History: The Life of Joseph Smith, the Mormon Prophet*. New York: Alfred A. Knopf.

Brooks, J. 1950. *The Mountain Meadows Massacre*. Stanford, CA: Stanford University Press.

Brown, S. 2020. *Joseph Smith's Translations: The Words and Worlds of Early Mormonism*. New York: Oxford University Press.

Bushman, R. 2005. *Joseph Smith: Rough Stone Rolling*. New York: Alfred A. Knopf.

Bushman, R. 2023. *Joseph Smith's Gold Plates: A Cultural History*. New York: Oxford University Press.

Bushman, C. L. 1997. *Mormon Sisters: Women in Early Utah*. Logan, UT: Utah State University Press.

Campbell, C. 2004. *Images of the New Jerusalem: Latter Day Saints Faction Interpretations of Independence, Missouri*. Knoxville, TN: University of Tennessee Press.

Colvin, G. and J. Brooks. 2018. *Decolonizing Mormonism: Approaching a Postcolonial Zion*. Salt Lake City, UT: University of Utah Press.

Conkin, P. 1990. *Cane Ridge: America's Pentecost*. Madison, WI: University of Wisconsin Press.

Coviello, P. 2019. *Make Yourselves Gods: Mormons and the Unfinished Work of American Secularism*. Chicago, IL: University of Chicago Press.

Davis, I. 1934. *The Story of the Church: A History of the Church of Jesus Christ of Latter Day Saints, and of Its Legal Successor, the Reorganized Church of Jesus Christ of Latter Day Saints*. Independence, MO: Herald Publishing House.

Daynes, K. 2001. *More Wives than One: The Transformation of the Mormon Marriage System, 1840–1910*. Urbana, IL: University of Illinois Press.

Driggs, K. 1991. Twentieth Century Polygamy and Fundamentalist Mormons in Southern Utah. *Dialogue: A Journal of Mormon Thought* 24: 44–58.

Duffy, J. and D. Howlett. 2016. *Mormonism: The Basics*. New York: Routledge.

Edwards, P. 1988. *The Chief: An Administrative Biography of Fred M. Smith*. Independence, MO: Herald House.

Farmer, J. 2008. *On Zion's Mount: Mormons, Indians and the American Landscaping*. Cambridge, MA: Harvard University Press.

Fenton, E. and J. Hickman, eds. 2019. *Americanist Approaches to the Book of Mormon*. New York: Oxford University Press.

Flake, K. 2005. *The Politics of American Religious Identity: The Seating of Senator Reed Smoot, Mormon Apostle*. Chapel Hill, NC: University of North Carolina Press.

Flanders, R. 1965. *Nauvoo: Kingdom on the Mississippi*. Urbana, IL: University of Illinois Press.

Fluhman, S. 2012. *A Peculiar People: Antimormonism and the Making of Religion in Nineteenth Century America*. Chapel Hill, NC: University of North Carolina Press.

Foster, C. L. and M. Watson. 2019. *American Polygamy: A History of Fundamentalist Mormon Faith*. Charleston, SC: The History Press.

Givens, T. 2002. *By the Hand of Mormon: The American Scripture that Launched a New World Religion*. New York: Oxford University Press.

Givens, T. 2017. *Feeding the Flock: The Foundations of Mormon Thought: Church and Praxis*. New York: Oxford University Press.

Givens, T. 2007. *People of Paradox: A History of Mormon Culture*. New York: Oxford University Press.

Givens, T. 2015. *Wrestling the Angel: The Foundations of Mormon Thought: Cosmos, God, Humanity*. New York: Oxford University Press.

Gordon, S. B. 2002. *The Mormon Question: Polygamy and Constitutional Conflict in Nineteenth Century America*. Chapel Hill, NC: University of North Carolina Press.

Hales, Br. 2006. *Modern Polygamy and Mormon Fundamentalism: The Generations after the Manifesto*. Salt Lake City, UT: Greg Kofford Books.

Hardy, B. C. 1992. *Solemn Covenant: The Mormon Polygamous Passage*. Urbana, IL: University of Illinois Press.

Hardy, G. 2010. *Understanding the Book of Mormon: A Reader's Guide*. Oxford: Oxford University Press.

Harper, S. C. 2019. *First Vision: Memory and Mormon Origins*. New York: Oxford University Press.

Harris, M. L. and N. Bringhurst. 2016. *The Mormon Church and Blacks: A Documentary History*. Urbana, IL: University of Illinois Press.

Hendrix-Komoto, A. 2022. *Imperial Zions: Religion, Race and Family in the American West*. Lincoln, NE: University of Nebraska Press.

Holland, D. F. 2011. *Sacred Borders: Continuing Revelation and Canonical Restraint in Early American*. New York: Oxford University Press.

Hollinger, D. 2022. *Christianity's American Fate: How Religion Became More Conservative and Society More Secular*. Princeton, NJ: Princeton University Press.

Homer, M. 2014. *Joseph's Temples: The Dynamic Relationship between Freemasonry and Mormonism*. Salt Lake City, UT: University of Utah Press.

Howard, R. 1969. *Restoration Scriptures: A Study of Their Textual Development*. Independence, MO: Dept. of Religious Education, Reorganized Church of Jesus Christ of Latter Day Saints.

Howlett, D. 2007. The Death and Resurrection of the RLDS Zion: A Case Study in "Failed Prophecy," 1930–70. *Dialogue: A Journal of Mormon Thought* 40: 112–31.

Howlett, D. 2014. *Kirtland Temple: A Biography of a Shared Sacred Space.* Urbana, IL: University of Illinois Press.

Howlett, D. 2020. Why Denominations Can Climb Hills: RLDS Conversions in Highland Tribal India and Midwestern America, 1964–2001. *Church History: Studies in Christianity and Culture* 89: 3, 633–58.

Hunt, L. 1982. *F.M. Smith: Saint as Reformer.* Independence, MO: Herald House

Hurlbut, D. D. 2018. The LDS Church and the Problem of Race: Mormonism in Nigeria, 1946–1978. *International Journal of African Historical Studies* 51: 1–16.

Hurlbut, D. D. 2015. *Nigerian Converts, Mormon Missionaries, and the Priesthood Revelation: Mormonism in Nigeria, 1946–1978.* Boston, MA: Boston University Working Papers in African Studies.

Hutchison, W. 1992. *The Modernist Impulse in American Protestantism.* Cambridge, MA: Harvard University Press.

Inouye, M. 2014. The Oak and the Banyan: The Glocalization of Mormon Studies. *Mormon Studies Review* 1:1, 70–9.

Jenkins, P. 2009. Letting Go: Exploring Mormon Growth in Africa. *Journal of Mormon History* 35: 1–25.

Johnson, J. 2023. *Convicting the Mormons: The Mountain Meadows Massacre in American Culture.* Chapel Hill, NC: University of North Carolina Press.

Kerns, V. 2021. *Sally in Three Worlds: An Indian Captive in the House of Brigham Young.* Salt Lake City, UT: University of Utah Press.

Kline, C. 2022. *Mormon Women at the Crossroads: Global Narratives and the Power of Connectedness.* Urbana, IL: University of Illinois Press.

Larson, G. O. 1971. *The Americanization of Utah for Statehood.* San Marino, CA: Huntington Library.

Launius, R. 1995. Coming of Age: The Reorganized Church of Jesus Christ of Latter Day Saints in the 1960s. *Dialogue: A Journal of Mormon Through* 28: 31–57.

Launius, R. 1988. *Joseph Smith III: Pragmatic Prophet.* Urbana, IL: University of Illinois Press.

LeSeuer, S. 2011. *The 1838 Mormon War in Missouri.* Columbia, MO: University of Missouri Press.

Linn, W. 1902. *The Story of the Mormons from the Date of Their Origin to the Year 1901.* New York: Macmillan.

MacKay, M. M. H. 2020. *Prophetic Authority: Democratic Hierarchy and the Mormon Priesthood.* Urbana, IL: University of Illinois Press.

Marsden, G. 1977. Everyone One's Own Interpreter? The Bible, Science, and Authority in Mid-Nineteenth Century America. *History of Education Quarterly* 17: 17–30.

Marsden, G. 1995. *Fundamentalism and American Culture*. New York: Oxford University Press.

Marty, M. E. and S. Appleby, eds. 1995. *Fundamentalisms Comprehended*. Chicago, IL: University of Chicago Press.

Mauss, A. 1994. *The Angel and the Beehive: The Mormon Struggle with Assimilation*. Urbana, IL: University of Illinois Press.

McDannell, C. 2018. *Sister Saints: Mormon Women since the End of Polygamy*. New York: Oxford University Press.

McLoughlin, W. G. 2013. *Revivals, Awakenings and Reform*. Chicago, IL: University of Chicago Press.

Mohrman, K. 2022. *Exceptionally Queer: Mormon Peculiarity and U.S. Nationalism*. Minneapolis, MN: University of Minnesota Press.

Mueller, M. P. 2017. *Race and the Making of the Mormon People*. Chapel Hill, NC: University of North Carolina Press.

Newell, Q. 2019. *Your Sister in the Gospel: The Life of Jane Manning James, a Nineteenth-Century Black Mormon*. New York: Oxford University Press.

O'Brien, H. 2023. *Irish Mormons: Reconciling Identity in Global Mormonism*. Urbana, IL: University of Illinois Press.

Park, B. 2020. *Kingdom of Nauvoo: The Rise and Fall of a Religious Empire on the American Frontier*. New York: Liveright.

Petrey. T. 2020. *Tabernacles of Clay: Gender and Sexuality in Modern Mormonism*. Chapel Hill, NC: University of North Carolina Press.

Porterfield, A. 2012. *Conceived in Doubt: Religion and Politics in the New American Nation*. Chicago, IL: University of Chicago Press.

Prince, G. and W. Wright. 2005. *David O. McKay and the Rise of Modern Mormonism*. Salt Lake City, UT: University of Utah Press.

Pulido, E. E. 2019. *The Spiritual Evolution of Margarito Bautista: Mexican Mormon Evangelizer: Polygamist Dissident, and Utopian Founder, 1878–1961*. New York: Oxford University Press.

Quinn, D. M. 1985. LDS Church Authority and New Plural Marriages, 1890–1904. *Dialogue: A Journal of Mormon Thought* 18: 9–105.

Quinn, D. M. 1994. *The Mormon Hierarchy: Origins of Power*. Salt Lake City, UT: Signature Books.

Reeve, W. P. 2014. *Religion of a Different Color: Race and the Mormon Struggle for Whiteness*. New York: Oxford University Press.

Reiss, J. 2019. *The Next Mormons: How Millennials Are Changing the LDS Church*. New York: Oxford University Press.

Riley, I. W. 1902. *The Founder of Mormonism: A Psychological Study of Joseph Smith*. London: William Heinenmann.

Roberts, B. H. 1930. *Comprehensive History of the Church of Jesus Christ of Latter-day Saints*. Salt Lake City, UT: Deseret News Press.

Rosetti, C. 2024. *Joseph White Musser: A Mormon Fundamentalist*. Urbana, IL: University of Illinois Press.

Rosetti, C. 2022. Not Until the Millennium: 1978 and Fundamentalist Whitelash. *American Religion* 3: 51–68.

Russell, W. 2008. *Homosexual Saints: The Community of Christ Experience*. Ann Arbor, MI: John Whitmer Books.

Shepherd, G. and G. Shepherd. 2015. *A Kingdom Transformed: Early Mormonism and the Modern LDS Church*. Salt Lake City, UT: University of Utah Press.

Shepherd, G., G. Shepherd, and R. Cragun, eds. 2020. *The Palgrave Handbook of Global Mormonism*. London: Palgrave Macmillan.

Shields, S. 2022. *Divergent Paths of the Restoration: An Encyclopedia of the Smith-Rigdon Movement*. Salt Lake City, UT: Signature Books.

Shipps, J. 1985. *Mormonism: The Story of a New Religious Tradition*. Urbana, IL: University of Illinois Press.

Shipps, J. 2007. Richard Lyman Bushman, the Story of Joseph Smith and Mormonism, and the New Mormon History. *Journal of American History* 94: 498–516.

Simpson, T. W. 2016. *American Universities and the Birth of Modern Mormonism, 1867–1940*. Chapel Hill, NC: University of North Carolina Press.

Smith, J. Jr. 1856. *The History of the Church of Jesus Christ of Latter-day Saints*. Salt Lake City, UT: Church of Jesus Christ of Latter-day Saints.

Smith, J. III, and H. C. Smith. 1897. *The History of the Reorganized Church of Jesus Christ of Latter-day Saints*. Lamoni, IA: Board of Publication of the Reorganized Church of Jesus Christ of Latter Day Saints Herald Publishing House and bookbindery.

Speek, V. 2006. *God Has Made Us a Kingdom: James Strang and the Midwest Mormons*. Salt Lake City, UT: Signature Books.

Spencer, J. M. 2023. *A Word in Season: Isaiah's Reception in the Book of Mormon*. Urbana, IL: University of Illinois Press.

Staker, M. 2011. *Hearken, O Ye People: The Historical Setting of Joseph Smith's Ohio Revelations*. Salt Lake City, UT: Greg Kofford Books.

Stapley, J. 2018. *The Power of Godliness: Mormon Liturgy and Cosmology*. New York: Oxford University Press.

Stegner, W. 1992. *The Gathering of Zion: The Story of the Mormon Trail*. Lincoln, NE: University of Nebraska Press.

Stone, D. 2018. *William Bickerton: Forgotten Latter Day Prophet.* Salt Lake City, UT: Signature Books.

Strong, J. 1885. *Our Country: Its Possible Future and Present Crisis.* New York: American Home Missionary Society.

Turner, J. G. 2012. *Brigham Young: Pioneer Prophet.* Cambridge, MA: Harvard University Press.

Ulrich, L. T. 2017. *A House Full of Female: Plural Marriage and Women's Rights in Early Mormonism.* New York: Alfred A. Knopf.

Walker, D. 2019. *Railroading Religion: Mormons, Tourists, and the Corporate Spirit of the West.* Chapel Hill, NC: University of North Carolina Press.

Wright, S. A. and S. Palmer. 2016. *Storming Zion: Government Raids on Religious Communities.* New York: Oxford University Press.

New Religious Movements

Founding Editor

†James R. Lewis
Wuhan University

The late James R. Lewis was a Professor of Philosophy at Wuhan University, China. He was the author or co-author of 128 articles and reference book entries, and editor or co-editor of 50 books. He was also the general editor for the *Alternative Spirituality and Religion Review* and served as the associate editor for the *Journal of Religion and Violence*. His prolific publications include *The Cambridge Companion to Religion and Terrorism* (Cambridge University Press 2017) and *Falun Gong: Spiritual Warfare and Martyrdom* (Cambridge University Press 2018).

Series Editor

Rebecca Moore
San Diego State University

Rebecca Moore is Emerita Professor of Religious Studies at San Diego State University. She has written and edited numerous books and articles on Peoples Temple and the Jonestown tragedy. Publications include *Beyond Brainwashing: Perspectives on Cultic Violence* (Cambridge University Press 2018) and *Peoples Temple and Jonestown in the Twenty-First Century* (Cambridge University Press 2022). She is reviews editor for *Nova Religio*, the quarterly journal on new and emergent religions published by the University of Pennsylvania Press.

About the Series

Elements in New Religious Movements go beyond cult stereotypes and popular prejudices to present new religions and their adherents in a scholarly and engaging manner. Case studies of individual groups, such as Transcendental Meditation and Scientology, provide in-depth consideration of some of the most well known, and controversial, groups. Thematic examinations of women, children, science, technology, and other topics focus on specific issues unique to these groups. Historical analyses locate new religions in specific religious, social, political, and cultural contexts. These examinations demonstrate why some groups exist in tension with the wider society and why others live peaceably in the mainstream. The series highlights the differences, as well as the similarities, within this great variety of religious expressions. To discuss contributing to this series please contact Professor Moore.

For EU product safety concerns, contact us at Calle de José Abascal, 56–1°,
28003 Madrid, Spain or eugpsr@cambridge.org.

www.ingramcontent.com/pod-product-compliance
Ingram Content Group UK Ltd.
Pitfield, Milton Keynes, MK11 3LW, UK
UKHW020207240325

456635UK00018B/286